'Wood's book gives us one of the most valuable analyses of Putin's personality and motives that I have read to date. Although authored by leading scholars, it is an easily understood book for the intelligent layperson. It is also terrifying. We often tend toward projecting some rationality onto dangerous autocrats or even denial of their severe intractable psychopathology. However, this book argues that there is "government by dangerous, strongmen figures driven by insatiable appetites, deeply compromised empathy, and a very destructive form of narcissistic pathology – that represents a clear and present danger the world must soon find a way to contend with if human survival is to be protected... that it is a danger that is growing, as witness the rise in autocracies around the world, and a danger that history tells us has resulted in unimaginable human suffering and ecological damage." I want influential government officials to read this book, not only to understand Putin, but to understand and never underestimate the malignant autocrat that is ready to destroy all that is good in society. Wood's book should be taken as a very serious warning.'

Robert M. Gordon, PhD ABPP, *licensed Psychologist,*
Diplomate of Clinical Psychology, Diplomate of Psychoanalysis,
Governing Council, American Psychological Association

'The contributions rendered in this book provide invaluable insight, enlightened perspectives and deep understanding of the etiology, manifestation and psychodynamics of the toxic strongman leader who has historically rendered, and is currently inflicting incalculable harm, if not also annihilation, upon his fellow human beings. There is equally penetrating attention given to those he has seduced into toxic followership. There is much to learn and take away from each of these erudite authors' offerings. It is a wake up call. The geopolitical landscape is changing and the threat that such leaders present to our way of life is of ever-increasing magnitude. It must be clearly defined, well understood and immediately countered, not only by our political leaders, military chiefs, intelligence agencies and academics, but by an engaged citizenry – that is, all of us.'

Tim Gilmore, *Psychologist,*
Gilmore Associates

'This is a book about the frightening world created by Vladimir Putin. It includes attempts by the author Richard Wood and his fellow psychoanalyst Brent Willock to understand Putin's mind, its development, and how that development has contributed to the behaviour that has come to frighten the world.

Willock draws attention to the impact of adverse childhood experiences on personality development and as the root cause of most social, economic, and mental health issues, including violence. He characterizes Putin's psychopathology as arising from a Kleinian paranoid schizoid perspective preceding the capacity for concern. He describes the frighteningly empty life of a schizoid personality, covering the lost heart of the self with psychopathic armour. Putin and other totalitarians provide themselves with an illusory sense of power, safety, independence, and esteem.

The possibility that Putin was born illegitimately to a woman other than the mother, described in his autobiography and noted by Willock, is an interesting piece of information since, if true, it offers a potentially altered view of his early development and possible evidence of a serious attachment disorder. Attachment pathology has shown individuals to develop either intense need for relatedness (anaclitic pathology) or narcissistic and antisocial behaviour (introjective pathology: Blass et al. 1998).

Three of the chapters in the book do not address Putin's psychopathology directly. Coline Covington, a training analyst and political philosopher, addresses the reasons for Putin's invasion of Ukraine. In a delightful chapter she writes of Putin's perception of a Eurasian Russia pitted against all Western democracies, seen as enemies, bent on destroying Russia, and as a threat to Putin's defensive need for total control of others. She paints a picture of a dangerous man who should not be dismissed as a bluffer.

Ian Hughes writes of the pathologies of the historical developments of modernity. This excellent article outlines how science and knowledge and the seventeenth-century industrial revolution changed 2,000 years of struggling to survive for 85% of the world's population into better lives. Unfortunately, this still leaves 15% of the population starving and barely surviving.

The benefits of new knowledge and better standards of living have led to democracies, the abolition of slavery, and greater individual freedoms. Hughes also addresses the factors that oppose democracy, namely the rise of dictatorships with accompanying kleptocracy, hyper masculinity, debasement of women, loss of individual freedoms, and the inability to express personal feelings and ideas, all of which are features of Putin's Russia.

James Merikangas is a neuroscientist who offers possible biological explanations for Putin's psychopathy. The author describes the effect of the Treaty of Versailles on German society and their embrace of Hitler and his atrocities. He also addresses the atrocities conducted by the allies in retaliation. He suggests that we have moved from the age of "mutually assured destruction" to "nuclear blackmail" in Putin's invasion of Ukraine. Merikangas hopes that a scientific understanding of the brain will meld neurobiology with psychology and shape child development and education. In his view the study of figures like Napoleon, Stalin, Hitler, and Putin remains important if we are to survive the nuclear age.

Wood believes that malignant narcissism is a unitary diagnosis that can be conceived as a subclass of psychopathy. His comprehensive description of the condition derives from a childhood in the care of a malignant narcissist father and his subsequent professional experience of psychodynamic psychotherapy with narcissistic patients. Both add to the credibility of Wood's formulation. In the case of Putin, while questions might be raised about the merits of diagnosis from a distance, there is so much verified information about the behaviour of this political leader that conclusions can be drawn. The evidence of complete lack of empathy, ruthless destruction of opponents, and the absence of real friendships instructs us about potential future behaviour. A book such as this goes beyond professional interest. In the context of the ongoing war in Ukraine it will provide those who hope to end war and restore peace useful information about what they can and likely cannot expect from Putin as they attempt to negotiate with him.

For mental health professionals, the introductory and closing chapters of the book describe a psychodynamic understanding of Putin's psychopathology and his development – development that exposed him to poverty and abuse, all dangers to a nascent self. By training in martial arts as a youth to adult membership in the KGB, Putin aimed to protect his sense of self. Others' independent selves are dangers to be eliminated.

This book will be appreciated by psychoanalysts, psychologists, and psychiatrists alike. The additional chapters will also appeal to political scientists, historians, and journalists and politicians, not to mention the general public.'

David Raymond Freebury, *Associate Professor of Psychiatry, University of Toronto*

'Richard Wood's *Psychoanalytic Reflections on Vladimir Putin: The Cost of Malignant Leadership* brings a vast array of psychological and psychoanalytical knowledge to the study of the Russian president. It's an extremely erudite, insightful, and well-written study, providing the reader with many valuable perspectives, including by several additional thoughtful authors. I strongly recommend it to deepen your understanding of Putin and the West's relationship with him.'

Dr. Paul H. Elovitz, *Presidential Psychobiographer, Research Psychoanalyst, Editor-In-Chief of* Clio's Psyche, *and Director of the Psychohistory Forum*

Psychoanalytic Reflections on Vladimir Putin

Psychoanalytic Reflections on Vladimir Putin: The Cost of Malignant Leadership attempts to explore the core psychodynamics that appear to characterize Vladimir Putin's presidency.

Its contributors examine the nature of the leader-follower relationship, the costs of malignant leadership, and the larger historical context in which Putin's presidency is unfolding. The sobering threat of nuclear war is considered. Finally, the viability and ethics of distance assessment are discussed.

This book will be of great interest to psychoanalysts and to readers seeking to understand the complex dynamics of populist leadership.

Richard Wood, PhD, is a psychoanalytically oriented clinical psychologist based in Ontario, Canada, with over 45 years of experience. He is the author of *A Study of Malignant Narcissism* (Routledge).

Psychoanalytic Reflections on Vladimir Putin

The Cost of Malignant Leadership

Edited by
Richard Wood

LONDON AND NEW YORK

Designed cover image: Zephyr18 © Getty Images

First published 2024
by Routledge
4 Park Square, Milton Park, Abingdon, Oxon OX14 4RN

and by Routledge
605 Third Avenue, New York, NY 10158

Routledge is an imprint of the Taylor & Francis Group, an informa business

© 2024 selection and editorial matter, Richard Wood; individual chapters, the contributors

The right of Richard Wood to be identified as the author of the editorial material, and of the authors for their individual chapters, has been asserted in accordance with sections 77 and 78 of the Copyright, Designs and Patents Act 1988.

All rights reserved. No part of this book may be reprinted or reproduced or utilised in any form or by any electronic, mechanical, or other means, now known or hereafter invented, including photocopying and recording, or in any information storage or retrieval system, without permission in writing from the publishers.

Trademark notice: Product or corporate names may be trademarks or registered trademarks, and are used only for identification and explanation without intent to infringe.

British Library Cataloguing-in-Publication Data
A catalogue record for this book is available from the British Library

ISBN: 978-1-032-45408-5 (hbk)
ISBN: 978-1-032-43845-0 (pbk)
ISBN: 978-1-003-37681-1 (ebk)

DOI: 10.4324/9781003376811

Typeset in Times New Roman
by codeMantra

To my wife Mary, whose love fills my world, and to the many colleagues who offered their critical appraisals and insight to my work

Contents

Contributor Biographies		*xiii*
Credit List		*xv*
Acknowledgements		*xvii*
Prologue		*xix*
1	A Model of Malignant Narcissism RICHARD WOOD	1
2	Does the Model Fit Putin? RICHARD WOOD	16
3	Incredibly Wealthy, Catastrophically Impoverished (Regarding Humanity, Love, Empathy, Values): Whatever Happened to You, Vladimir Putin? BRENT WILLOCK	53
4	The "Empire of Lies": Russia's War in Ukraine COLINE COVINGTON	69
5	The Leader-Follower Relationship RICHARD WOOD	79
6	Vladimir Putin and the Pathologies of Modernity IAN HUGHES	92
7	Nuclear Blackmail JAMES R. MERIKANGAS	101

Summary

105

RICHARD WOOD

Epilogue

115

RICHARD WOOD

Index

119

Contributor Biographies

†**Dr. Coline Covington**, PhD, BPC, PSA, received her BA in Political Philosophy from Princeton and then moved to the UK where she received her MPhil in Criminology from Cambridge and her PhD in Sociology from the LSE. She worked for nearly ten years as a consultant with criminal justice agencies throughout England and set up the first UK mediation project between victims and juvenile offenders with the Metropolitan Police in London.

Coline was a training analyst of the Society of Analytical Psychology and the British Psychotherapy Foundation and former chair of the British Psychoanalytic Council. She is a fellow of International Dialogue Initiative (IDI), a think tank formed by Prof. Vamik Volkan, Lord Alderdice, and Dr. Robi Friedman to apply psychoanalytic concepts in resolving political conflict. From 2011 to 2013, Coline was Visiting Research Fellow in International Politics and Development at the Open University and Senior Scholar at the Woodrow Wilson International Center for Scholars in Washington, DC. Coline has written extensively on political morality from a psychoanalytic perspective, including her trilogy Everyday Evils: *A Psychoanalytic View of Evil and Morality (Routledge, 2017), For Goodness Sake: Bravery, Patriotism and Identity (2020), and Who's to Blame? Collective Guilt on Trial* (Routledge, 2023).

Coline was in private practice until her untimely death on July 17, 2023, in London, UK.

Dr. Ian Hughes, PhD, is a scientist and author. He is a senior research fellow at the MaREI Centre, Environmental Research Institute, University College Cork, Ireland and a policy advisor on science, technology, and innovation policy. His book *Disordered Minds: How Dangerous Personalities Are Destroying Democracy* explores how a small proportion of people with dangerous personality disorders are responsible for most of the violence and greed that mars our world. He is currently leading the Deep Institutional Innovation for Sustainability and Human Development (DIIS) initiative at University College Cork.

James R. Merikangas, MD, is a neuropsychiatrist, co-founder of the American Neuropsychiatric Association, and former president of the American Academy of Clinical Psychiatrists. He is a graduate of the Johns Hopkins University School of Medicine and trained in both neurology and psychiatry at Yale. Currently he is Clinical Professor of Psychiatry and Behavioral Science at the George Washington University School of Health Sciences and a consultant in research at the National Institutes of Mental Health. An interest in the causes and prevention of violent behaviour led to the evaluation of more than 200 murderers. He has pioneered the use of brain imaging in the understanding of violent crimes.

Dr. Brent Willock, PhD, CPsych, majored in psychology at McGill University, then earned his doctorate in clinical psychology from the University of Michigan. After being on staff for several years in the Department of Psychiatry at the University of Michigan Medical Center, he relocated to Toronto, becoming chief psychologist at a clinical facility associated with the University of Toronto. He was an adjunct faculty, York University, and an associate faculty member, School of Graduate Studies, University of Toronto. He is the past president of the Toronto Institute for Contemporary Psychoanalysis and serves on the Board of the Canadian Institute for Child & Adolescent Psychoanalytic Psychotherapy. He is a faculty member in the Postgraduate Program in Psychoanalysis and Psychotherapy at Adelphi University's Derner School of Psychology, writing mentor for the Washington Psychoanalytic Foundation's New Directions in Psychoanalytic Thinking Program, and associate editor for *Psychoanalytic Dialogues*, and has contributed many book chapters and articles. He is author of *Comparative-Integrative Psychoanalysis and The Wrongful Conviction of Oscar Pistorius*, and has edited several books that received Gradiva and Goethe Awards. His many contributions have been honored by the Ontario Psychological Association, the American Psychological Association, the Canadian Psychological Association, the International Federation for Psychoanalytic Education, the University of Chicago, the Chicago Institute for Psychoanalysis, and the National Association for the Advancement of Psychoanalysis.

Credit List

The authors also gratefully acknowledge the permission provided to reprint excerpts from the following materials.

Excerpt(s) from *The Man Without a Face: The Unlikely Rise of Vladimir Putin* by Masha Gessen, copyright © 2012 by Masha Gessen. Used by permission of Riverhead, an imprint of Penguin Publishing Group, a division of Penguin Random House LLC. All rights reserved.

The Man Without a Face: The Unlikely Rise of Vladimir Putin by Masha Gessen, Granta Publications.

The Road to Unfreedom by Timothy Snyder, Penguin Random House.

Putin by Philip Short © Philip Short, 2022, published by Bodley Head, reproduced by kind permission by David Higham Associates.

Vladimir Putin by Michael Eltchaninoff, Hurst Publishers.

Who's to Blame? Collective Guilt on Trial, 1st edn, Chapter 8, Coline Covington, Routledge, Taylor & Francis Group (Coline Covington's chapter included in this book is reprinted from this text published by Routledge, Taylor & Francis Group).

The New Tsar: The Rise and Reign of Vladimir Putin by Steven Lee Myers, Vintage Books (a division of Penguin Random House, LLC, New York), Paperback ISBN: 978-0-345-80279-8, © 2015 Steven Lee Myers.

Acknowledgements

A book can never be a solitary endeavour but, rather, the product of a community of effort that manifests itself through direct contribution or through indirect, and often poorly understood, influence others exert upon us. That is perhaps especially true of an edited book. So many conversations and ideas passing back-and-forth between collaborators, some of them not directly affiliated with the book as authors. I count myself very privileged to be able to draw upon numbers of colleagues whose ideas I value who are willing to be very honest with me about my work and who readily set aside time to offer me their appraisals of the chapters I contributed. Every one of them had suggestions to make – important suggestions – that I incorporated into the chapters that I wrote. Some of them undertook the painstaking work of checking for grammatical and punctuation errors as well. My friends and colleagues Brent Willock, Ray Freebury, Ian Hughes, Tim Gilmor, and Bob Gordon were such people. I thank them for their wisdom and for the pleasure, once again, of being able to work together. My voice in this book is both my own and a composite of theirs. It truly has been a privilege to undertake this task together.

I also owe a great deal of thanks to my wife, Mary Walton, who has endlessly helped me carry out my research, listened to my rants about computer problems and glitches (solving most of them for me), and offered her editorial advice about my writing, which one ignores at their peril (she is almost inevitably right about changes I need to make to the manuscript). She also has provided comfort, support, encouragement, and enormous patience as I moved through my journey, which was not always an easy one. My debt to her is immeasurable.

I owe an almost equal debt to Mary's daughter, Melanie Ryan, who has both accepted me as family and devoted considerable time and resource to this book, fastidiously checking the manuscript for errors and formatting it so that it could be rendered acceptable to Routledge. She has shared her ideas as well, providing me with insightful, useful perspectives and a supportive, caring presence.

And finally, I owe many thanks to my editor at Routledge, Susannah Frearson, who helped me navigate through what was, at times, a fairly fraught process with equanimity, tolerance, more than a measure of forbearance, and the willingness to re-formulate the project at a critical juncture in time. I have worked with Susannah before and know that I can count on her to see me through a challenging writing process.

Prologue

The publication of *The Dangerous Case of Donald Trump* ignited passionate discussion within the mental health professions about practitioners' right to "diagnose" a sitting national leader even though they had not carried out direct clinical examination of him or her. As Editor of this book, that question was foremost in my mind when I considered embarking on this project. I knew that my authors and I would be attempting to understand facets of Vladimir Putin's personality so that we could better appreciate a leader whom we believed was causing great harm to the worldwide community. Our focus was not upon judgement but rather upon insight that we hoped we could generate in a dispassionate, respecting way – insight, we believe, that is essential to us if we are to understand why pathological leadership has been so persuasive throughout much of human history.

Our focus, then, was not just to be on Putin but also on ourselves. What is it about the human character that draws us to cling to strong men who profess to know better than we do how to navigate our way through the frightening landscape that is often life. Answering those questions certainly meant looking at Mr. Putin; the answers we seek also require us to examine who we are. Accordingly, some of the chapters in this book will explore Mr. Putin's putative formative life experiences and psychodynamics (Drs. Willock and Wood); others will consider facets of the leader-follower relationship, including the vulnerabilities we carry within us that lead us to accommodate ourselves to the often destructive saviors we endow with leadership responsibility (Drs. Covington and Wood). Some of our writers will explore the viability of carrying out distance assessments (Drs. Willock and Wood). Others will examine broad historical themes as they intertwine with intrapsychic ones that together seem to have shaped what is taking place within Russia and its interface with the rest of the world (Drs. Hughes and Covington). Still other writers – Drs. Merikangas, Covington, and Wood – will direct some of their attention towards the terrible risks that the war creates for all of us.

The ensuing portrait of the events now unfolding not just in Ukraine, but on a world-wide stage that we attempt to construct in this book is grounded in psychological and psychoanalytic science. We also make assiduous attempts to marry psychoanalytic insights with the salient historical realities and themes that Putin's biographers have so ably investigated. As such, this book can be regarded as a confirmation of the importance that we believe close acquaintance with both history and psychology plays in understanding human affairs. History needs the expertise that psychological sciences offer and psychological sciences, in turn, need the painstaking construction of historical facts and speculation that historians are capable of. Even though clinicians like psychoanalyst Dr. Paul Elovitz have laboured for decades in the field he and others refer to as psychohistory, this arena of scholarship has yet to enjoy the vigorous and widespread focus of investigation that I would say is very much needed, given some of the contemporary challenges we face.

In preparation for writing this book, many of our authors have read widely about Putin, turning to the extensive, fine biographies numbers of historians and an investigative reporter have provided. In our most aspirational moments, we would wish that this book could serve as a compelling invitation for more historians to join with their colleagues in the psychological sciences in appraising and understanding the human story unfolding both around us and within us.

More should be said about the difficulties of distance evaluation. Even under the best of circumstances, what we can know as mental health practitioners about people that we work with must inevitably be limited by the nature of the science that we employ. For those of us who engage in psychotherapy practices, we are daily reminded that in exploring the mysteries of human existence we can at best only offer approximations of the truth that we attempt to capture in our work with patients. That same limitation must also define the historian's work. In spite of the welter of facts that can be affirmed and circumstances that can be described that attend historical events, trying to capture the essence of the personality the historian means to investigate using the best means he has at his/her disposal is always fated, in some important respects, to produce an imperfect and certainly incomplete appraisal. That is certainly the nature of social science endeavour. We use the best means that we possess to make sense of that which we think we are seeing consistent with the standards and methodologies that contemporary social science knowledge affords us. As is incumbent for us to do, we outline our methodologies, review our data analysis, and render the pathways to the conclusions we draw accessible and transparent. We always take care to ensure that the reader understands our grasp of what we are seeing is potentially flawed. We expect ourselves to remind our readers and our colleagues that there may be other, better explanations that can be employed to capture the realities we're trying to understand. Indeed, "knowing" is a humbling process, confirming for us again and again that ideas that once captivated us require amendment and/or reinterpretation. That is certainly true of our patient work as we find ourselves reappraising, reframing, and reformulating as a treatment process unfolds. As a treatment relationship deepens, new information emerges that prompts us to reconsider what we thought we knew about a given individual. If we're lucky, we move ever closer to a meaningful grasp of what someone's life experience has meant to them and of the ways in which it might have affected them.

None of us have had the means to work with Vladimir Putin in a treatment context, nor is he likely to afford us or himself such an opportunity. Accordingly, none of us have had the chance, with his help and collaboration, to carry out a deep exploration of his personal life experience over an extended period of time, appraising and reformulating our ideas as new vistas present themselves to both us and our prospective patient. Each of our writers who comments about Putin has struggled with this conundrum. That struggle will be quite manifest in some of the chapters that readers of this book will encounter. This has been a topic that many of us have discussed together and often at quite some length. The best that we can do is identify the data that we're referencing, the methodologies of data analysis that we use, and the conclusions that we draw in a highly transparent manner. Each of us, in turn, recognizes that, in the end, our colleagues will help us make sense of the adequacy of our work and our ideas as they offer their own commentary about what we have done. In this sense, we are deeply interdependent upon one another in any scientific undertaking, awaiting the help and the fresh perspectives that our colleagues can bring to bear on our work.

Many of the tools and especially concepts that we rely upon to carry out distance assessment, as the reader will see, we are already closely familiar with. In that sense, the new ground that we break is very much informed by an array of means that have characterized various aspects of our past investigations of human personalities. We hope to forge – with the passage of time – clearer consensus about how distance assessment can be undertaken. That is certainly one of the reasons why I invested in this project and invited others to do so – apart, of course, from a pressing need to know more about Putin and other leaders like him.

It was as a consequence of the Goldwater Rule, which was conceived by the fraternal body representing the American Psychiatric Association, that practitioners were first asked not to comment upon diagnosis unless they had directly examined a patient. Because this rule originated in a fraternal body, rather than a regulatory one, it was/is not binding on psychiatrists. Other mental health professionals, in turn, do not face similar limitations imposed by either their fraternal or regulatory bodies and so are conceivably free to engage in various forms of distance assessment. As Dr. Robert Gordon will point elsewhere (pending publication), distance assessment as part of forensic psychological assessment has established itself as a viable assessment methodology that has been tested over a very considerable period of time in courts in a broad variety of venues. He notes that in-person assessment and psychological testing are both likely to generate a distorted portrait of personality if the person being examined is defined by strong psychopathic tendencies. Moreover, unlike patients who come to us for help and have a vested interest in participating in a collaborative, exploratory process that may produce discomfort for them, attempts to explore Putin's psychological realities may well be dangerous for the assessor, as witness the many members of the media who have been jailed or faced assassination under his tenure. Because of his strong concern about the need for distance assessment, Dr. Gordon and his colleagues have made assiduous efforts over a course of years to develop a distance assessment tool based upon the Psychodiagnostic Chart-2 (PDC-2). The resulting instrument is simple to use and is possessed of strong reliability, validity, and utility (see Gordon et al, 2016). It does, however, require the expertise of clinicians familiar with constructs that the Mental Function Scale of the PDC-2 embraces. In Gordon's soon-to-be-published study, 50 experienced clinicians evaluated the psychological health of Vladimir Zielinski, Vladimir Putin, and Donald Trump using the PDC-2. Both Putin and Trump scored in an impaired range, while Zielinski's functioning was deemed to fall in a healthy range. There was strong interrater reliability and the differences between Trump and Putin's functioning were seen to be statistically significant, even though both seemingly demonstrated impairment in critical psychological capacities. Gordon and his colleagues' breakthrough work may prove to offer us potential means to carry out distance assessment in a reliable, meaningful way.

Notwithstanding the absence of regulatory limitations preventing distance assessments and their broad use in certain contexts, many practitioners remain concerned about carrying out distance assessment. It is a practice that very understandably raises a number of pressing ethical questions that practitioners are implicitly expected to struggle with, understanding that they can be asked to provide a rationale for the choices that they have made in any given set of circumstances.

Offsetting concern about distance assessment, as implied in the very first paragraph of the prologue, is growing, deep uneasiness about the impact that pathological leadership is having upon the human condition. At present, 57 nations in the world are dominated by dictators encompassing as much as 70% of the world's population. Freedom House, a watchdog organization that oversights the measure of freedom that people living in different countries in the world enjoy, cautions us that in the last 15 years we have moved from a position in which three people out of five could be said to living in more or less free societies to a situation in which approximately one in five does now. In response, some practitioners, at least, are feeling pressure to bring their knowledge to bear on this age-old problem, educating both the public and themselves about a challenge that many feel may be fatally compromising the human endeavour. For some mental health professionals, in other words, there is a growing sense of urgency to be forthcoming about what we have learned and share it so that we speak out effectively about potentiality of harm. Not an easy set of choices to face.

Those of us who practise psychoanalytically, like other "depth" mental health practitioners, have the opportunity to see, as our years of work with patients unfolds, that personalities we found reprehensible, offensive, frightening, or morally repugnant are just people struggling with oft-times horrific damage in their own lives they have neither the means nor the opportunity to rectify. As much as it may be comfortable to rail against the injustices that people direct against their fellow humans, essentially separating ourselves from the ugliness we see around us and within us, in the end what we learn is both humbling and sobering. That's not to say that we become immune to our own rage and indignation (that doesn't happen).

Like everybody else we're playing injured, sometimes doing a better job of it than at others. And like everybody else, our imperfections assail us at every turn. That is why it is so essential for the reader to keep in mind that Vladimir Putin is one such person with a history and a story that, if fully understood, would most likely generate compassion and understanding. Even in the context of such a depth of understanding, however, we may simultaneously find ourselves feeling a deeply disconcerting mix of responses and emotions that also defines any relationship we might have with him, either directly or through the agency of daily news feeds.

I would say that in part the profound uneasiness we feel towards him may be a reflection, however distantly experienced, of our uneasiness with dark aspects of our own interiors. We all turn off empathy to protect ourselves, even if in so doing we harm others. We all, in one form or another, subject others to the kind of pain that we have experienced ourselves. And we have all acted in self-interested ways or indulged rage and envy in a fashion that compromises the people around us. We can't – and mustn't – look at Putin's without also looking at ourselves. This book represents an attempt to explore some of the dark spaces we all have in common with one another even though this darkness afflicts some of us to a greater extent than others. The intention is to treat the subject matter we are addressing with gravity and respect; it is not meant to represent vilification of a man who ultimately represents a tragic figure, though one capable of causing great injury to our human community. We argue that as we understand him and ourselves better, we can better divert ourselves from those whose pain ruinously connects to our own.

Reference

Gordon, R.M., Blake, A., Bornstein, R.F., Gazzillo, F., Etzi, J., Lingiardi, V., … & Tasso, A.F. (2016). What do practitioners consider the most helpful personality taxa in understanding their patients? *Division/Review: A Quarterly Psychoanalytic Forum*, 16, 70.

Chapter 1

A Model of Malignant Narcissism

Richard Wood

In this chapter, I will describe the model of malignant narcissism that I presented in my book, *A Study of Malignant Narcissism: Personal and Professional Insights*. In the chapter which follows, I will attempt to assess whether the model "fits" Putin's behaviour as it has been described by historians and an investigative journalist as well as Putin himself. I will ask the reader to assume a sceptical, critical stance, looking for evidence that either confirms or disconfirms the model I have conceived.

Before embarking on a description of the model of malignant narcissism that I have pieced together, it is fitting to acknowledge that much of the framework I constructed rests on the conceptions of many clinicians who proceeded me. I would like now to briefly review core concepts other clinicians have articulated through their work with patients they considered to be malignantly narcissistic and/ or through their analysis of pathological leadership.

It's important to underscore that the construct "malignant narcissism" represents relatively new science and, as such, is conceived of in different ways by different practitioners. There is real disagreement about whether it ought to be considered a unitary concept, an intersection of different personality disorders, or even as alternate forms of disorder that would not be seen to fall under the rubric of malignant narcissism. Clinicians who see it as an intersection of different personality disorders constitute the majority position of scientific opinion. Fromm, in his ground breaking work *The Heart of Man*, suggested that the concept malignant narcissism, which he introduced in 1964, was the consequence of a confluence of forces that included pathological narcissism, investment in processes that opposed life-giving and life-expanding activities (a necrophilous orientation), and what he referred to as incestuous symbiosis (an intense desire to surrender selfhood and personal responsibility by joining with a powerful other). Kernberg (1984), somewhat in contrast, who also wrote extensively about malignant narcissism, saw it as a confluence of pathological narcissism, psychopathy, predilection to cruelty, and paranoid personality disorder. Other practitioners, like Hughes (2018, 2019), Malkin (2017), Gartner (2017), and Stone (2018) largely adopted his perspective. Burkle (2016) believed that the destructive personalities that he was attempting to describe represented a regression from pathological narcissism to antisocial personality disorder. Viewing

DOI: 10.4324/9781003376811-1

the same set of behaviours (Donald Trump's) that had led some practitioners to conclude that what they were seeing was malignant narcissism, Tansey (2017) saw delusional disorder, Friedman (2017) identified paranoid character structure, and Dodes (2017), sociopathy. Only Mika and Shaw (2014) were of the opinion, as I am, that what they were looking at was a unitary personality disorder.

Most authors seemed to agree that what they were seeing was a particularly dangerous, destructive variant of the human character that could potentially produce dramatic injuriousness to the human community. Fromm referred to malignant narcissism, simply, as "evil." Lists of pathological leaders that various clinicians were inclined to regard as representing the destructive traits they were attempting to understand included Stalin, Hitler, Mao, Pol Pot, Putin, Trump, Milosevic, and Kim Jong un. Mika asserted that all tyrants "are predominantly men with a specific character defect, narcissistic psychopathy (a.k.a. malignant narcissism)" (2017, p. 290). In my book, I maintained that the limited number of malignant narcissists I had worked with clinically were all male as was, of course, my father, whose autobiographies and interactions with me provided a major focus for my investigation of malignant narcissism.

In spite of their differences, clinicians repeatedly identified the same foundational blocks or core psychodynamics that appeared to characterize these personalities. Central to clinicians' portraits was rigid reliance upon a grandiose, omnipotent self that provided cohesiveness which, variously, protected the narcissist against identity dissolution (Kernberg, 1975), underlying depression (Fromm, 1964), or mortification or psychic death by shame (Shaw, 2014). Kernberg (1975) argued that having assured themselves of their own grandiosity and perfection, malignant narcissists could protect themselves against ever having to acknowledge their need for other people. Shaw (2014) believed that the malignant narcissist, which he referred to as traumatizing narcissism, erected rigid, manic defences that disavowed susceptibility to dependence which had occasioned painful, shame-inducing attacks during formative years. In his analysis of Trump, Gartner (2017) alluded to hypomanic temperament. Kernberg noted that malignant narcissists demonstrated an inability to experience sadness, mournful longing, and depression as a "basic feature of their personalities" (1970, p. 53). All authors endorsed deeply impaired empathy, envy, oral rage or rage (referencing out-of-control appetites), profound entitlement, unyielding self-interest that ensured the narcissist occupied an increasingly solitary world, paranoia, sadism, contempt, intolerance of individuality, and a desire to subvert, invade, or control others' subjectivity. There was also general agreement that the psychodynamics that characterizes this dangerous group of people severely compromises rationality and judgement; appraisal of reality is readily displaced by the dictates of narcissistic needs and injuries. Malkin (2017) warned that "a psychotic spiral" (p. 56) could ensue if life events challenged the malignant narcissist's ascendancy – a spiral that would be marked by intensifying paranoia, projection, increasing lapses of judgement, escalating need to impress others, volatile decision-making, and gaslighting. Mika (2017) believed that malignant narcissists were fated to deconstruct themselves eventually because of the way they were organized as personalities. Kernberg (1970) conceived of malignant narcissism as a defence against borderline fragmentation. He concluded that malignant narcissism, like Borderline Personality Organization, incorporated the same basic defences (splitting, projection, projective identification, idealization/denigration). In his description of the defensive structures sociopaths employ, Dodes (2017) drew attention to projective identification and splitting, suggesting that the former could be seen to be a process in which the impulses or attributes projected into another person are experienced as being sufficiently dangerous that the sociopath feels impelled to mount an attack.

Of all the clinicians that one read, Kernberg (1970) provided the most extensive portrait of what the inner world of the malignant narcissist might look like. He felt that it was largely devoid of good objects – representations of sustaining and rewarding relationships – and was instead defined by idealized representations of the self, "shadows" of the people the malignant narcissist had exploited in his attempts to feed himself, and dreaded enemies. In a particularly poignant passage, Kernberg described a "hungry, enraged, empty self full of impotent anger at being frustrated, and fearful of the world which seems as hateful and revengeful as the patient himself" (p. 57). In his view, narcissistic defences were constructed to protect this emaciated core.

There appeared to be relatively wide disagreement about the etiological factors that set the stage for malignant narcissism and related conceptions, like paranoid disorder and psychopathy. Most etiological conceptions, moreover, did not appear to be widely supported by extensive case material and most appeared to be propositional rather than articulated in depth. Kohut (1976) referenced specific kinds of empathic failures that he thought might elicit narcissistic adjustment. Kernberg (1970) admitted that

> it is hard to evaluate to what extent (the development of pathological narcissism) represents a constitutionally determined strong aggressive drive, a constitutionally determined lack of anxiety tolerance in regard to aggressive impulses, or severe frustration in their first years of life.
>
> (p. 58)

He also speculated that chronically cold parental figures possessed of intense covert aggression could be expected to characterize the histories of malignant narcissists. Shaw (2014) placed emphasis on shaming as causative. Hughes (2018) noted, simply, that early environments fostering love and fun enhanced humanity while those marked by hate, fear, and abuse undercut potential for humanity and decency. Mika (2017) advanced the idea that

> it is impossible to rule out narcissistic upbringing as being involved in raising a future tyrant – creating a narcissistic injury that shaped the child's life and

4   Richard Wood

set him on a path of 'repairing' it through ruthless and often sadistic pursuit of power and adulation – even when there is no evidence of overt abuse and/or neglect in his biographical data.

(pp. 291–292)

In my book, I conceived of malignant narcissism as arising from specific forms of trauma – most particularly, but not exclusively, severe early parentification which demanded that a child focus nearly exclusive attention upon parental need while their own needs were being either ignored or debased. In response, the child becomes implacably mistrustful, anticipating rapacity from others rather than love or generosity. I also imagined that identification with a malignant narcissistic posture could arise in response to the devastation and starvation of self that ensues as the self is repeatedly exposed to predation from a narcissistic other, particularly if the narcissistic personality undertaking predation demands that the personality being predated attempts to emulate the "strength" and the various qualities of the narcissistic invader. In such a context, the alternative to identification is continued devastation and emaciation of selfhood that literally feels like the self is being annihilated. My childhood experience growing up with a malignantly narcissistic father revealed yet another path to malignant narcissism, the one that I nearly found myself taking: psychic emaciation; an inner life increasingly populated with sadistic, malevolent imagery; endemically high levels of fear; and profound, pervasive dissociation increasingly stood in the way of decency, of connection to others, and of a capacity to appreciate others' pain. I recognized, as did many of the practitioners I referenced in the preceding discussion, that there are many potential etiologies that may lead to malignant narcissism, including pathogenic and genetic ones (see James Merikangas' chapter on nuclear threat). My intention was to elucidate those which my own life experience had revealed to me as best I could, using the rich case material that my encounters with my father and my reactions to him offered me. My father had also provided me two very lengthy autobiographical statements at my request. In addition, I had access to 46 years of patient work, a small part of which included extended work with patients I considered to be malignantly narcissistic as well as shorter-term work with either this group of patients and/or their family members.

As I pieced together my own formulation of malignant narcissism and the dynamics that seemed to define it, I argued that malignant narcissism appears to be a subclass of psychopathy. I also wondered, given the clinical picture that I saw emerging as I explored malignant narcissism, whether it might more properly be classified as a trauma disorder – that is, as a form of disorder that arises in response to profoundly injurious trauma experience. Within the context of the trauma perspective, one would anticipate that an affected individual would continuously re-enact their trauma in various forms until they somehow enjoyed resolution of the injuries they had endured. I suggested that the form of trauma implicated in malignant narcissistic personality structure would properly be classified as a form of complex posttraumatic stress syndrome – like malignant narcissism, a propositional diagnosis, one not formally incorporated into clinical practice.

Our current conceptions of complex posttraumatic stress disorder (CPTSD) acknowledge that complex PTSD occasions profound disruption of core, foundational developmental processes because, by definition, the trauma starts early in people's lives and is continuous rather than a single event (as in the case of PTSD). This is often the case with an abusive parent. Research has shown that CPTSD creates much more damage to the self and to the capacity for mutually satisfying intimacy than many other forms of trauma disorder, creating substantial, persistent challenges that extend well throughout one's lifespan (Cloitre et al., 2013). Rather than being subjected to a painfully intrusive thought process in which traumatic imagery repeatedly imposes itself in an unbidden way, the malignant narcissist is able to spare himself this pain by acting it out, or externalizing it, and imposing it on others. Unless what I am calling malignant narcissistic personality disorder is subject to substantial amelioration, I posited that it tends, over a lifetime, to escalate the damage it imposes on the self and on others who find themselves targeted by a very destructive presence. Such people, in other words, tend to become more dangerous and more damaging as they age. My reasons for taking such a position will become more apparent as the discussion below unfolds.

While concepts like complex posttraumatic stress disorder have not yet been recognized in the diagnostic manual in common currency, the DSM-5, appreciation of the lasting impact of complex developmental trauma is a foundational part of psychoanalytic thought. Complex posttraumatic stress disorder (CPTSD) has been included as a diagnostic category in the International Classification of Diseases, 11th Edition. The PTSD diagnosis in *ICD-11* consists of the following symptoms: re-experiencing the traumatic event(s); avoidance of thoughts, memories, activities, etc. that serve as reminders of the event; and persistent perceptions of heightened current threat. Individuals are considered to have complex PTSD if they meet these symptoms and in addition endorse (1) affect dysregulation, (2) negative self-concept, and (3) disturbed relationships. Complex PTSD is recognized by the United States Department of Veterans Affairs (VA) and the National Health Service (NHS).

As I emphasize in my book, using the word malignant is not meant to connote judgement or revulsion, but, rather, recognition of the extraordinary damage that malignant narcissistic personalities in positions of leadership and responsibility can inflict on others. Personalities like Mao, Stalin, and Hitler can be conceived of as malignant narcissists who have occupied leadership positions as heads of state. Robert Gordon (unpublished manuscript) documents the terrible costs that their leadership has occasioned within the human community. It is not my point of view that the people we might describe as malignant narcissists are abhorrent aberrations of the human character wc can dissociate ourselves from because we wish to think of them as being so different than we are ourselves; on the contrary, I am appealing to my readers to recognize that we all carry significant potentiality for malevolence within ourselves, malevolence that we must understand and recognize so that we don't enact it, as the followers of malignant narcissistic leaders do with such terrible efficiency.

Central to my formulation was the idea that malignant narcissistic personality organization evolves because it creates safety for the afflicted individual in response to profound early trauma. "Safety" is afforded through assumption of a grandiose, omnipotent self that confirms that one is protected from early incursions the world imposed which the self experienced as unbearable. Safety asserts itself as the strength to dominate and suborn others rather than being exploited and overpowered in turn. By implication, such a personality has faced so much repeated, intolerable violation and threat that it must insulate itself against its own humanity, ensuring that it remains untouched by interactions that require vulnerability and openness to others. In the process, deeply rewarding, sustaining interactions that require empathy, compassion, respect for others, conduct mediated by decency, and a willingness to let others in one's world touch one deeply all face compromise. Authenticating others' voices is a profoundly threatening undertaking. Strength means shutting others down and usurping their place, confirming, in the process, that the self never has to endure rapacity and humiliation. The investment in dominating others and keeping them out is rigid and unyielding; cracks in the wall threaten the aggrandized self that is deemed, at least unconsciously, to be essential for survival. Any real or perceived attack upon the aggrandized self produces reflexive and ruthless counterattack meant to devastate the other. Relentless vindictiveness may ensue. Moreover, such behaviour can and often does emerge in response to seemingly small sleights, objectively out of all proportion to the injury being sustained. In such a context, love becomes increasingly improbable inasmuch as it not only requires but incites celebration of others' individuality and their uniqueness. The malignant narcissist is therefore living in a solipsistic world, one defined by their own voice, their own emotional vicissitudes, their own needs, and their own prerogatives of action. It is a profoundly lonely, isolating place, but one that offers insulation against a world the malignant narcissist has learned – through unendurably painful experience – is malevolent.

The malignant narcissist's life posture reflects imposing – and one would say, unyielding – mistrust of other people. Such mistrust requires formidable walls meant to keep other people out, providing reassurance that others cannot obligate through bonds of fealty and affection. Relationships become largely transactional, defined by others' capacity to help the narcissist satiate their own needs. Very few people get inside and stay inside the narcissist's inner circle for long and those that do cannot lay claim to friendship defined by openness, warmth, playfulness, and intimate knowledge of the other. The narcissist rarely lets down his guard and rarely lets other people establish emotional purchase in his life. Friendship, inasmuch as it exists, is deeply constrained by the narcissist's fear of weakness and his imposing mistrust. More typically, transactional interactions typify his exchange with others; so long as mutuality of interest remains compelling, a relationship persists; when utility dissipates, relationships can end with startling abruptness. Close love relationships with a loving partner quickly become unsustainable; genuine intimacy requires far too much vulnerability. It also entails that one is relatively comfortable expressing dependent yearnings that the narcissist would find both repugnant and terribly compromising to his core defences. The narcissist must protect himself both against the urge to love others and to be loved in return. In lieu of relationship, the narcissist craves conquest, risk-taking, confirmation of his prowess, and superficial allure in the object of his interest, none of which can satisfy him for long, producing a restless, bored relationship style that may expose him to multiplicities of "partners," none of whom can truly participate in a genuinely loving collaboration with him because his defences prevent him from doing so. More often than not (but not always), partnerships are based upon their transactional value to the narcissist. Partners who are genuinely loving and decent eventually become intolerable for the malignant narcissist, who may depreciate them and deconstruct them before moving on to others less threatening for him to accommodate.

The implacable mistrust which pervades malignant narcissistic adjustment means that the malignant narcissist must continually test his relationships. He does not have access to confirmation of a friendship's or a love relationship's viability that arises because two people can directly experience their depth of affection for one another. In addition to their transactional value, his relationships work for him because of others' willingness to accommodate themselves to his voice and to the manifestations of his will. Anyone whose personality becomes too well articulated begins to cross a line that incites rage and excoriation; independence of thought and action challenge essential narcissistic prerogatives and, by implication, the narcissist's survival. For the narcissist to exist comfortably in the world, his voice must be the biggest and most commanding voice, one that in the end everyone must accommodate themselves to, enacting his choices and his prerogatives. No one's voice, in other words, can remain bigger or more prominent than the narcissistic voice for long. The offending personality must be neutered, humiliated, or, if the offense is felt to be subjectively grievous enough, erased. Enactment of sadistic retaliation confirms potency. Sadism also enables aliveness and a sense of engagement with life in lieu of loving engagement with others.

As a result of the dynamics that I've just described, the narcissist's interpersonal world is rather precarious, largely confirmed by acts of power and domination. The narcissist must demonstrate to himself that others will drink the Kool-Aid whenever he needs them to. They must show him that they can accommodate his shifting perspectives and prerogatives without raising meaningful challenge. They must also endure the humiliation that he inflicts on them as a means of confirming his dominance, even and perhaps especially when a given counterattack he initiates can be seen to be arbitrary or disproportionate. In such a fashion the malignant narcissist shows himself over and over that the people around him are prepared to bend themselves to his needs. He is most likely to choose people as his close colleagues who are not only willing to take on his voice as required, but whose own moral or criminal failings reassure him that he has devastating leverage to turn against them should they betray him.

8 Richard Wood

Repeatedly violating others provides reassurance in the moment that all is as it should be, or as he prefers, with his world. In the long run, however, invading and subverting others further deepens mistrust, rendering the world an ever more dangerous place for him – and one that requires renewed and intensified efforts to assure himself of dominance in an environment in which, at some level, he appreciates he is making more and more enemies. His mistrust means that people move in and out of his world with surprising rapidity, some of whom are permanently ejected and others of whom face "redemption" of sorts after they are disqualified. Ultimately, the real point is that nobody can get too close or stay very close for too long. Relationships are utilitarian and they are characterized by formidable emotional distance. No one gets to touch the malignant narcissist in a personal way over an extended period. No one can lay claim to him or obligate him. He cannot allow the formation of personal connections that compel him. He builds formidable barriers between himself and other people that often assume the form of withering contempt, humiliation, and implied or real threat. Ultimately, people are "things" to be used to consolidate power and authority, to meet his own often poorly understood but consuming needs, and to be tested endlessly to show him that they are willing to dance to the tune that he plays.

Conducting his interpersonal relationships in the way that he does means that he can never satiate himself and fill himself with that which truly sustains people: mutuality of regard, warmth, playfulness, spontaneity, acts of decency, depth of affection, and behaviour informed by genuine concern for the other rather than the self. In consequence, the malignant narcissist is starving. The walls that he builds to keep others out and ensure that they cannot meaningfully touch him also prevent him from obtaining the supplies of nurturance that would relieve him of his insatiable, restless hunger – nurturance that would otherwise potentially provide him with a sense of meaning, the possibility of place in the broader human community, and a genuine sense of well-being and safety. More simply put, if one can't give, one can't get. Starvation produces rage and envy, inflaming the malignant narcissist's voracious, out-of-control needs. Rage that is never far from the surface and that can be easily harnessed by the narcissist's eternal, hair trigger vigilance. In effect, the narcissist, as my colleague Ian Hughes (personal communication) has pointed out, is perpetually envious of love itself – love that he can't give and that he can't receive. Stuffing himself with a glut of power, status, money, and fame never really satisfies; it can't begin to meet the human needs that he requires himself to deny in order to protect himself. Accommodating those needs would require him to relinquish the very life lines that he depends upon to keep him afloat: his omnipotence and grandiosity, his objectification of the people around him, and a posture demarcated by ruthlessness and "strength."

Ever mistrustful, continuously hypervigilant, always on the lookout for others' malevolent intent, the malignant narcissist inevitably creates devastating injury to those he experiences as enemies. Increasingly, his internal life becomes populated with dark images of predation, cruelty, and envy, creating a blighted internal wasteland populated by images of the ugliness that he enacts and that he experiences. He would see his darkness as confirmation of power, as evidence that he can emerge ascendant in a world that would otherwise brutalize him. He idealizes his ruthlessness, presenting it to the world around him as a desirable attribute that, he would argue, serves to protect people under his care. Inevitably, his own darkness escalates the devastated landscape inside, further exacerbating the starvation he must endure. Humanity recedes further. Cruelties compound themselves. Cruelty and risk-taking, as I have noted earlier, become the means through which he can make himself feel alive and engaged, however temporarily. Even his sadism, however, may eventually fail to reward him, as he becomes bored with his casual dispensation of death (Kernberg, 2003, p. 953).

His internal world increasingly consolidates his perception of the external world as being characterized by malicious intent. In this fashion, he comes to live in a projected world, one defined by his expectation that others can be expected to be as rapacious as he is. Boundaries between what he experiences and that which others experience become increasingly permeable. Others become imbued with the same toxic intentionality that defines him. He projects his world with its attendant ugliness on to others, expecting that they would act as he acts. He accuses them, in other words, of being as voracious, ruthless, and greedy as he is himself, all the while arguing that he only does what he must in order to fend off those who attempt to encroach on him and dominate him. Under the worst of circumstances, he can become quite paranoid, either inflating or anticipating risk of attack that is out of all proportion to the risk that a given context creates for him. In such circumstances, he can act pre-emptively and dangerously, much as Lance Dodes (2017) has suggested. His cunning intelligence harnesses the deep cynicism his view of others occasions, relying on it to provide justification for the entitlements he wishes to consummate to feed his unquenchable appetites. As I noted in my book, the malignant narcissist also sometimes capitalizes upon the threat that his malevolence creates in others as a means of overpowering them – he appreciates, in other words, that others find his darkness deeply disconcerting and deeply uncomfortable, turning away from it rather than confronting him and pushing back. His feral intelligence equips him well to read others' vulnerability and hesitation, which he would experience as weakness to be exploited and opportunity to be fulfilled. In such circumstances his attribution of toxicity to the other is a conscious tactic that not only justifies his subsequent aggressive actions, but also serves to convey potent intimidation.

Broadly speaking, genuine difficulties distinguishing between what he is feeling and what others are feeling is part of a process in psychoanalytic literature referred to as projective identification; he not only projects his feelings and intentions onto others, but in attacking them or threatening them, gets them to act and feel in the way that he does, providing substantiation for his original perceptions. Conscious misattribution of blame, on the other hand, is referred to as blame shifting. Both are foundational processes in malignant narcissism. What renders them confusing is the way in which the malignant narcissist can shift back and forth between largely unconscious process (classic projective identification) and relatively conscious ones (varying levels of blame shifting), both of which can be embodied in a single exchange with him. Traditionally, projective identification and blame shifting can be seen to serve the function of ejecting the "bad" or destructive aspects of the self onto and into others, thus sparing the self a catastrophic confrontation with its most repellent parts. It can be seen from the foregoing discussion, however, that protection against the bad self often recedes in importance as projective identification and/ or blame shifting (or both) serve various important transactional functions such as establishing and justifying entitlements, creating threat, eroding the selfhood of the other, obfuscating the malignant narcissist's intentionalities, impression managing followers' perceptions, etc. Sorting through propositional motivations associated with both defensive operations can clearly be quite daunting at times.

Splitting is another core defensive operation believed to be a seminal part of malignant narcissistic personality organization. Splitting works in close conjunction with projective identification and blame shifting. Splitting allows the individual enacting this defence to break the world of people up into binary schemas that permit one to apply gross, sweeping generalizations to others that render them either inordinately good or inordinately bad. Within my formulation of malignant narcissism, splitting, too, can be associated with differing levels of conscious intent. At one end of the spectrum, the other who has been targeted by this defence is experienced as profoundly repugnant or extraordinarily decent. At the other, transactional motivation assumes more prominence as perception of the other is deliberately manipulated to serve a particular end. Deliberate, conscious defamation of a group of people may help consolidate unity in a larger group that the malignant narcissist wishes to exploit; it could be relied upon to generate high levels of threat and fear in society at large that renders its members more malleable; it could be used to punish a group of people that the malignant narcissist sees as standing in the way of his rapacities; it could permit the malignant narcissist to disguise and deflect attention away from other targets and other interests, etc. Like projective identification and blame shifting, it can be immensely complicated to sort through, in a given instance, how a malignant narcissistic leader is using splitting, i.e., as a conscious or unconscious action. For the moment, I am content to use blame shifting to describe conscious use of projective identification and splitting, though part of me would prefer two separate terms for these two different contexts. I choose simplicity and parsimony because they allow me to avoid creating jargon.

The malignant narcissist's devastated internal life, his deep, unrelenting mistrust of others, and his abhorrence of vulnerability together mean that he stands apart from others' humanity and from his own; as a consequence, his humanity has to be simulated and contrived, curated in a fashion that makes it appear genuine even though there are rarely genuine points of connection with others. A stiff, mechanical, or wooden presentation, the absence of self-depreciating humour that might confirm shared humanity, and the absence of an engaging smile or infectious warmth might all attest to the contrivance that dominates these personalities. It's as if the music of every day human interchange that informs and directs much of our

A Model of Malignant Narcissism   11

action and our responsivity to one another is unavailable to them, like attempting to dance without being able to hear melody and rhythm. Depending upon the disposition of abilities that characterize a given narcissistic personality, contrivance can unfold with surprising effect, simulating relatedness with sufficient proficiency that the actor can wear a number of different faces, each one potentially as convincing as a last. Elizabeth Mika has observed that, for the malignant narcissist, empathy means discerning what one's listeners want to hear and then offering it.

Often relatively raw, unmitigated acts of impulsivity coexist with contrivance, creating an uneven, discordant tableau punctuated by orchestration and chaos. One could speculate that the press of both immense need, immense rage and envy, and immense entitlement must result in impulsive acts, sometimes explosively expressed. In my original conception, impulsivity was as prominent a part of malignant narcissistic presentation as contrivance.

Both because the narcissist's internal world and the external one are imbued with immense threat, he finds himself on a continuous war footing. Indeed, perpetual combat is necessary for the malignant narcissist to reassure himself that he can dominate the forces he experiences as assailing him and/or that he imagines might initiate attack. Only by demonstrating to himself and others that he is bigger, badder, better, more ruthless, and more cunning than the other can he create momentary safety for himself. In the process, however, the list of enemies that press against him grows ever larger. The necessity to be prepared to engage in combat becomes more imposing. Antipathy surrounds him. He is, however, exceptionally well prepared for the warfare he must face and that, often in substantial part, he has created. His intolerance of weakness and vulnerability means that he has had to learn how to shut down empathy in order to protect the self. Freedom from empathy, in turn, facilitates an action oriented, no holds barred assault when he experiences threat or when he wishes to exploit others through an aggressive exchange. Warfare, actual or figurative, is what he does best. It is the common currency of his exchange with others and with himself. Its aim is simple: obliteration of the targeted other in much the same way that he obliterates those who raise their voices persistently in objection to him. Combat and risk-taking also undoubtedly help contribute to aliveness and engagement. As such, the malignant narcissist may habitually seek them out, consolidating domination and grandiosity in the process.

I argued that the malignant narcissist – perversely – requires enemies in order to endlessly confirm for himself he is the undisputed King of the Hill. Combat is the language that he speaks best and that is most comfortable for him. So, too, is the language of threat. He promises safety for that part of his constituency that willingly twins itself with his desires. But he needs his constituents to be scared. Fear creates obeisance and pliability. Join with me, he seems to say, and you can bask sheltered by my strength and my grandiosity, safe from my wrath. He reminds the governed, however, that he can turn his anger towards others within the state, subjecting them to persecution, humiliation, and, worse, annihilation. Having targeted groups that he maligns within the state reminds everybody that nobody is really safe, that his reach is not to be denied. Endemically high levels of fear offer him opportunities to harvest people's worst impulses, redirecting them in a way that suits him best, further consolidating control.

Perpetual war footing and perpetual combat comes at a high cost. Psychological literature attests to the significant constraints that the malignant narcissist's enduringly high levels of fear arousal must have upon cognition. Thinking become simplistic, dividing events and people into binary categories (enabling splitting) that belie actual realities; nuance and discernment are replaced by the need to differentiate friend from foe. The language of fear driven cognition is visceral and guttural rather than measured and thoughtful. It depends upon emotional invocation rather than invocation of reason and temperance. It impels the bearer to act and to act in an unconstrained way to make sure that a source of threat is reckoned with quickly and mercilessly. So it is with the malignant narcissist and those who must live within the world that he creates (I will say more about his effect on the governed in a later chapter). There are other costs as well, especially on the fragile remnants of humanity that he still retains. Continuous threat produces dissociation, or emotional blunting, that further renders empathy and an awareness of harm more inaccessible. It becomes easier to injure and to do so without restraint the longer the malignant narcissist accommodates himself to the war environment he has generated.

As the malignant narcissist's dominion extends itself over time, growing mistrust and, on occasion, bouts of genuine paranoia incrementally erode what remains of his humanity, producing a personality that becomes increasingly solipsistic, reliant largely on its own authority and its own agency to address the complex problems which beset it and which only escalate in a context of perpetual alarm and aggression. Because the malignant narcissist is loath to rely on others and authenticate their voices, to an ever greater extent he becomes his own singular recourse to authority and to expertise; others' contributions and the gifts that they might bring him through collaboration become ever more unlikely resources for him to access. Already inclined to hyperbolize his own knowledge and expertise as a means of both muting others and testing their loyalty with the sometimes abrupt shifts in perspective that he imposes on them, his investment in his own irrational authority intensifies. Science and reason – particularly reason informed by compassion are displaced in favour of emotion-laden arguments given credence simply because they are deemed to serve the malignant narcissist's agendas. What matters is that he said it and felt it and would like others to say and feel what he does. Reason is depreciated because it stands in the way of his authority and his ability to arouse and manipulate the people he governs. As these patterns replicate themselves, his judgement becomes more and more tenuous and more detached from important realities that would otherwise require constructive attention. Solipsism and mistrust can be seen to set the stage for terrible miscalculations that occasion devastating human costs. They also increase the likelihood that he must eventually undercut his own credibility and, more importantly, his investment in his own grandiosity and omnipotence. Keep in mind that grandiosity and omnipotence are the linchpins that enable him to maintain the integrity of his identity. When increasingly extravagant errors of judgement occasioned by his isolation and his misappraisal of his own ability lead to crises that unseat his obdurate faith in himself, there is greater danger that his decisions will become proportionately more destructive to the human community – as did Hitler's invocation to German leadership to destroy industrial infrastructure in Germany to a degree that would have ensured impoverishment and social wreckage for generations to come.

Like Fromm and like Kernberg, I see malignant narcissism as a turning away from life and life-affirming activity towards impoverishment and death. The malignant narcissist, like the legendary vampire, is confined to a half-life, one in which he is eternally hungry, unable to nourish life in others, constrained instead to always take it in his desperate attempts to fill himself and create safety for himself that he can never have.

For ease of discussion, I will now simply list some of the salient features of malignant narcissism that I've identified so that the reader can compare and contrast my model of malignant narcissism with the salient characteristics of Putin's leadership. Once again, I would remind my reader to maintain an attitude of scepticism as they consider my formulation and my commentary. This is really new science, much like our still only tentative grasp of much of mental health knowledge, including the diagnostic categories that we rely upon. While many of the ideas and concepts that I have discussed have been documented by others (please see the extensive literature review which I have provided in my book), there is still a great deal of work to be done and many, many more conversations for us to have before we can place full faith in the ideas that we have been exploring and refining since the early 1900s. Like other writers in this book, I am of the view that we must begin to apply our knowledge of psychological dynamics to existing world leaders so that we are in a better position to identify extreme risk of harm. We do live in precarious times, after all. The future we all face could be said to be characterized by extreme danger, occasioned by climate change, risks to global health, extreme and growing wealth inequality, and ongoing warfare that we have not yet learned to live without.

Core characteristics of malignant narcissism could be said to include:

Severe early trauma that impels the individual to invest in ruthless, punitive forms of "strength" that offer protection against future violations

Investment in the conveyance of strength is a rigid, persistent, and relatively tenacious characteristic of the affected personality that can and often does extend itself throughout a lifetime

Manifestation of strength helps contribute to grandiosity and omnipotence that, increasingly, define malignant narcissistic identity, offering it the means to create cohesion and integrity in the face of traumatic early life experience

Re-enactment of early trauma

Significantly compromised empathy that supports an action-oriented, pull no punches, often brutal retaliatory response

Tenacious vindictiveness

Distant interpersonal relations that serve the function of protecting the affected individual from the encroachment and obligation love can impose

Relationships are marked by an absence of meaningful human engagement in which shared vulnerability, mutuality of respect, constructive interdependence, and the ability to elevate others' needs over one's own all remain out of reach

Very limited capacity to give and receive love

Contrivance of humanity and interpersonal exchange rather than genuine engagement informed by depth of meaning and attachment

Destruction of others' subjectivity, personhood, and voice

A presentation that is punctuated by episodically chaotic, impulsive acts

Both consciously and unconsciously driven forms of projective identification

Both consciously and unconsciously driven forms of splitting

A propensity to fulfil personal needs for inordinate power, wealth, status, and money with extraordinary ruthlessness

Insatiable appetites

An internal life characterized by blighted, destructive imagery

In the absence of meaningful amelioration, one expects significant deterioration of capacity for compassion and judgement over the malignant narcissist's lifespan.

References

Burkle, F.M. (2016). Antisocial personality disorder and pathological narcissism in prolonged conflicts and wars of the 21st century. *Disaster Medicine and Public Health Preparedness*, *10*(1), 118–128.

Cloitre, M., Garvert, D.W., Brewin, C.R., Bryant, R.A., & Maercker, A. (2013). Evidence for proposed ICD-11 PTSD and complex PTSD: A latent profile analysis. *European Journal of Psychotraumatology*, *4*(1), 20706.

Dodes, L. (2017). Sociopathy. In B. Lee (Ed.), *The dangerous case of Donald Trump* (2nd ed., pp. 78–87). New York: Thomas Dunne Books.

Friedman, H.J. (2017). On seeing what you see and saying what you know: A psychiatrist's responsibility. In B. Lee (Ed.), *The dangerous case of Donald Trump* (2nd ed., pp. 154–162). New York: Thomas Dunne Books.

Fromm, E. (1964). *The heart of man*. New York: Harper & Row.

Gartner, J.D. (2017). Donald Trump is: (A) bad, (B) mad, (C) all of the above. In B. Lee (Ed.), *The dangerous case of Donald Trump* (2nd ed., pp. 88–103). New York: Thomas Dunne Books.

Hughes, I. (2018). *Disordered minds: How dangerous personalities are destroying democracy*. Winchester, UK & Washington, DC: Zero Books.

Hughes, I. (2019). Disordered minds: Democracy as a defense against dangerous personalities. In B. Lee (Ed.), *The dangerous case of Donald Trump* (2nd ed., pp. 446–457). New York: Thomas Dunne Books.

Kernberg, O. (1970). Factors in the psychoanalytic treatment of narcissistic personalities. *Journal of the American Psychoanalytic Association, 18*, 51–85.

Kernberg, O. (1975). *Borderline conditions and pathological narcissism.* Lanham, MD: Rowman and Littlefield, Inc.

Kernberg, O. (1984). *Severe personality disorders.* New Haven, CO: Yale University Press.

Kernberg, O. (2003). Sanctioned social violence: Part II. *The International Journal of Psychoanalysis, 84*(4), 953–968.

Kohut, H. (1969–1970). On leadership. In P.H. Ornstein (Ed.), *The search for the self* (vol. 3, pp. 103–128). New York: Routledge.

Kohut, H. (1975). Remarks about the formation of the self. In P.H. Ornstein (Ed.), *The search for the self* (vol. 2, pp. 737–770). New York: International Universities Press, Inc.

Kohut, H. (1976). Creativeness, charisma, group psychology: Reflections on the self-analysis of Freud. In P.H. Ornstein (Ed.), *The search for the self* (vol. 2, pp. 743–843). New York: International Universities Press, Inc.

Malkin, C. (2017). Pathological narcissism and politics: A lethal mix. In B. Lee (Ed.), *The dangerous case of Donald Trump* (2nd ed., pp. 46–53). New York: Thomas Dunne Books.

Mika, E. (2017). Who goes Trump? Tyranny as a triumph of narcissism. In B. Lee (Ed.), *The dangerous case of Donald Trump* (2nd ed., pp. 289–308). New York: Thomas Dunne Books.

Shaw, D. (2014). *Traumatic narcissism.* New York & London, UK: Routledge.

Stone, M.H. (2018). The place of psychopathy along the spectrum of negative personality types. *Contemporary Psychoanalysis, 54*(1), 161–182.

Tansey, M.J. (2017). Why "crazy like a fox" versus "crazy like a crazy" really matters. In B. Lee (Ed.), *The dangerous case of Donald Trump* (2nd ed., pp. 88–103). New York: Thomas Dunne Books.

Chapter 2

Does the Model Fit Putin?

Richard Wood

Psychoanalytic theory posits that people inadvertently tell us about themselves through the way that they relate to themselves, to people around them, and the outside world. That axiom seems particularly true when people's behaviour is governed and shaped by the impact of trauma. Unless people have had the opportunity to ameliorate the harm that significant trauma has occasioned for them, they are likely to replay trauma in repetitive patterns that manifest themselves in subtle and obvious form; moreover, trauma patterns express themselves over and over again. Replaying formative trauma and conflict is seen to be immensely compelling. This concept is called repetition compulsion or, perhaps more precisely, traumatic re-enactment. As one of my colleagues who knew me early in my career told me, it's kind of like forcing yourself to watch a variant of the same play repeatedly until you finally understand it. Tragically, many people never do. Their defences kick in, protecting them from developing an awareness of the implications of their behaviour. Even when people are quite cognizant that they're suffering and/or causing others to suffer and even though they are quite aware that they need help, taking a look at the self can be quite challenging.

In addition to trauma-driven behaviour, people unconsciously construct habitual ways of thinking, feeling, acting, and being (what the PDM-2 refers to as personality syndrome) that grow out of the totality of their life experience, particularly early experience. Character structure is undoubtedly also shaped by the array of genetic givens/propensities that a particular individual carries within them. Character structure may be marked by inflexibility and rigidity, particularly when trauma informs the shape that character assumes. Trauma-informed character structure is also manifest in habitual patterns of relating, thinking, and feeling that typify a given individual. Such patterns can tell us a great deal about who people are.

As it happens, we have a particularly rich behavioural record that various historians and commentators have compiled about Vladimir Putin. This record not only includes both factual and speculative accounts of the various transactions in his life but also embraces an extensive record of other people's personal responses to Putin. Taken as a whole, the many volumes that have been written about Putin and the people who knew him provide an almost overwhelming fund of considered reflection about how he operates in the world and how he impacts the people

DOI: 10.4324/9781003376811-2

around him. The five writers that I have selected (Masha Gessen – *The Man Without a Face;* Timothy Snyder – *The Road to Unfreedom*; Philip Short – *Putin*; Steven Lee Myers – *The New Tsar: The Rise and Reign of Vladimir Putin*; Michael Eltchaninoff – *Vladimir Putin*) all have a professional commitment to weigh the material before them, as best they can, in a thoughtful and unbiased way. The sixth author that I have incorporated into my discussion is Putin himself. His semi-autobiographical book, *First Person*, also includes extensive commentary from people who knew him. Where substantial differences exist between writers, they will be noted, as much as that is possible within the scope of a relatively brief chapter.

What I propose to do is treat the record of Putin's behaviour as a fund of information that will enable me to begin to make sense out of who he is. Within the context of the framework I am using, it can be argued that it is hard for any of us to successfully hold all of our secrets, no matter how hard we might try. On my first day in graduate school in my very first class (psychopathology) my professor, who ended up becoming a mentor, began his relationship with us by telling us to "remember, people must inevitably convey what they are feeling themselves through the feelings and reactions that they evoke in you." He was trying to capture an axiomatic truth that, we would learn, was immensely complicated to apply. I do think that Putin has told us many important things about himself. The findings that my approach yields, however, must be regarded as propositional, as generating potentially very imperfect knowledge that may, nonetheless, help point us in important directions when we consider it in its totality. From my point of view, a psychoanalytic treatment context or possibly standardized testing or both would be ideal, but the quality of information that such processes yield depends heavily upon an individual's willingness to become a close collaborative partner in the endeavour. Such a possibility is clearly not to be realized in the current context.

It is essential as you read the commentary that I am about to offer that you remember I'm attempting to explore the psychic realities of a real person whose human journey is worthy of respect and compassion. Vladimir Putin is not the only leader to have drawn humanity into a catastrophic war or to have visited daunting suffering on his neighbours and the people that he governs. He is a focus of this work because we believe that we must attempt to understand the psychodynamics of those people who lead us badly and destructively. It is our hope that we can incite a broader, deeper conversation that will help us better appreciate not only that which we need to sidestep when choosing leaders, but that which should attract us as well. I will reemphasize a terribly important point that I raised in the first chapter: understanding leaders who cause us significant injury is not only about understanding them but understanding ourselves. History shows us that we have been willing to be led and led badly time and time again. Looking at leaders like Putin, then, means looking at ourselves and understanding our own sources of malevolence.

I will now consider whether the written evidence describing Putin's behaviour and people's response to him seems to confirm the salient features of my model of malignant narcissism. Even though I will attempt to discuss most of the prominent characteristics of narcissism separately, there will, of necessity, be some overlap in my discussion of the various categories and the written record; some of the behavioural examples that I cite may embody several malignant narcissistic markers. As much as possible, I'll try to remain focused on that aspect of malignant narcissism that I am directing attention to. My hope is that in so doing the discussion will be easier to follow. I would guess that readers will find themselves doing the same thing, i.e., seeing several different facets of malignant narcissism in a particular behavioural sample.

I should also emphasize that in citing evidence, I must inevitably rely upon the weighting and the appraisal of historical events that various writers, including those referenced by Putin's biographers, have provided. Sometimes such "evidence" will take the form of opinions and appraisals that others have offered; at other times, the portrait that I paint will derive from statements that people directly involved in the events I am describing have made. I do not have personal acquaintance, as someone like Masha Gessen does, with some of the personalities who have played a part, either directly or indirectly, in contemporary Russian history, nor have I had the advantage of talking to any of my sources directly. These are significant limitations which the reader must always hold in the forefront of their mind as they consider what I have to say.

Before proceeding with my analysis, it may be helpful to provide a limited amount of context for the reader so that the discussion which follows will be more understandable.

Both Putin's parents endured significant suffering and privation in the Second World War in the Leningrad theatre of operations, which may have represented one of the most brutal and costly battlegrounds of that conflict. His father absorbed wounds in ground combat operations that produced lasting impairment; his mother, as will be noted later in the discussion, not only lost one of her two children during the siege to diphtheria (Putin was to be her third child), but also nearly died herself, having been abandoned on a pile of corpses, mistaken for dead after passing out from the effects of starvation. Her first son, Albert, had died in his infancy before the war had begun; the second son, Victor, tragically contracted the diphtheria which killed him in a protected environment in Leningrad in which his mother had been told he would be safe. Putin was the "miracle child" who was born to his mother when she was 41. Both parents found employment for themselves after the war, his father as a tool maker in the Yegorov train car plant and his mother working as many as three jobs at one time to keep the family afloat financially. Like many other Leningraders, the family faced imposing postwar hardship, living in a dilapidated apartment building on Baskov Lane that was poorly heated and that was rat infested. The Putins shared a communal apartment consisting of three or four rooms and an inadequate kitchen and bathroom with two other families. Each family had a room of its own, with the possible exception of one of the families who may have split two very small rooms between the three of them. Putin's early adjustment to school and to academics was marred by behavioural challenges. As he matured, he became considerably more focused academically and demonstrated impressive discipline in his pursuit of excellence in his chosen sport, judo. Having been told that a career in law was most likely to win him selection by the KGB, which was a long-standing aspiration of his, he vigorously pursued admission to the Leningrad State University Law School and was successful in his efforts. In 1975, he was selected to join the KGB.

Strength and Intolerance of Vulnerability

The first characteristic of malignant narcissism that plays a central role in my conception of same is tenacious overvaluation of "strength" side-by-side intolerance for weakness and vulnerability. In Putin's case, the biographies suggest that investment in strength took the form of an almost compulsive, counter-phobic need both to seek out physical conflict and refusal to back away from it when threat presented itself.

Philip Short highlights Putin's commitment to a combative life stance in the following two passages:

> In later life, Putin wrote that he had been a hooligan as a child. Some of his contemporaries have argued that he was exaggerating to make it seem that his childhood had been tougher than it really was. It is true that, in the Soviet Union at that time, a hooligan was a criminal in the making and Putin did not take that road. But he was certainly a tearaway. The historian, Dimitri Raven, who also grew up in Leningrad in the 1960s, recounted: 'it wasn't so much that conflicts sought him out, it was he who was always looking for conflicts.' Whenever a fight broke out, Putin was the first to pile in. Viktor Borisenko, who became his best friend at school and for four years shared a desk with him, remembered: 'he could get into a fight with anyone. It still amazes me… He had no fear. He didn't seem to have an inner instinct for self-preservation. It never occurred to him that the other boy was stronger and might beat him up… If some hulking guy offended him, he would jump straight at him… Scratch him, fight him, pull up clumps of his hair… He wasn't the strongest in his class, but in a fight he could beat anyone because he would get into a frenzy and fight to the end.'
>
> (pp. 27–28)

Myers understood that

> by his own accounts and those of his friends, life in the courtyard and later in school made him rough, a brawler quick to defend against slights and threats, but it is more likely, given his size, that he was bullied.
>
> (p. 15)

20   Richard Wood

In another passage, Short again referred to Borisenko's appraisal of Putin:

> (Putin) liked brawling and hanging out with the local toughs in the courtyard but he was beginning to realize that it would bring diminishing returns. The atmosphere was terrible. Unshaven, dirty guys with port wine and cigarettes. Booze, obscene language, fights. And Putin was in the midst of all these bums. He wasn't a hoodlum himself, but he was constantly hanging out with them.
>
> (p. 39)

It was obvious, Short asserted, that many of them would end up in prison. But what concerned Volodya more, Short thought, was his own status:

> "To maintain the kind of leadership I had," (Putin) explained later, "it needed real physical strength and skills. I wanted to be able to keep that kind of leadership... I knew that if I didn't start sport, then in the courtyard and at school, I would no longer have the position that I was used to."
>
> (p. 39)

Subsequently, Putin involved himself in Sambo and, eventually, judo. Later Short pointed out that "in many ways Putin remained the same incorrigible youth that he had always been. He still got into fights, though less often than before. He still could not resist the challenge" (p. 46). In another subsequent passage, Short noted that "of his transition to a new school where he was to focus on chemistry, Putin and two other outsiders had to 'clarify matters' with their fists before their new classmates accepted them" (p. 48).

Myers believed that martial arts transformed Putin's life, "giving him the means of asserting himself against larger, tougher boys... It was a tool to assert himself in the pack." Myers, nonetheless, suggested that Putin's characterization of "his claim to live the life of the jungle sounded more like bravado" (p. 16).

In his own book, *First Person*, Putin explained that:

> I got into sports when I was about 10 or 11. As soon as it became clear that my pugnacious nature was not going to keep me King of the Courtyard or school grounds, I decided to go into boxing. But that didn't last long there. I quickly got my nose broken. The pain was terrible... Then I decided to go in for Sambo, a Soviet combination of judo and wrestling. Martial arts were popular at the time... At first I studied Sambo. Then judo.... Judo is not just a sport, you know. It's a philosophy. It's respect for your elders and for your opponent. It's not for weaklings...
>
> (p. 19)

In describing the death of his friend from a judo accident, Putin cautioned that "traumas like this were quite frequent during the competitions and matches. People would break their arms or legs. Matches were a form of torture. And training was hard, too" (p. 34).

In an important passage, Short reflected that "judo taught Putin that rather than resist a more powerful opponent, one should put him off balance and use his strength against him, making it possible for weaker opponents to beat significantly stronger ones." In such a fashion, Putin now had the means to offset vulnerability which his size occasioned for him (p. 60).

Judo culture, perhaps like the courtyard, exposed Putin to a brutish environment. Short reported that

> some of his childhood friends from the courtyard had gone on to a life of crime. In the judo clubs, he had been surrounded by criminals. Some of his friends had gone to prison and at least one of them was shot dead in a gangland funeral in St. Petersburg in 1994.
>
> (p. 181)

In addressing the question, "Did the KGB form Putin?" Short noted that "Putin himself is on the record as saying that much of what he was taught in the KGB, he already knew long before" (p. 93). Putin had understood through his KGB training that

> if something happens, you should proceed from the fact that there is no retreat. It is necessary to carry it through to the end. That's a well-known rule that was taught by the KGB, but I learned it much earlier, scrapping with the other kids. There was another rule the KGB taught. Don't reach for a weapon unless you are prepared to use it... It was the same on the street. (There) relationships were clarified with fists. You didn't get involved unless you are prepared to see it through.
>
> (p. 93)

Putin's boyhood friend Sergei Roldugin had been impressed by Putin's strength of character:

> Let's say I was a better soccer player. I would lose to him anyway, simply because he is as tenacious as a bulldog. He would just wear me down. I would take the ball away from him three times and he would tear it away from me three times. He has a terribly intense nature, which manifests itself in literally everything...
>
> (p. 51, *First Person*)

Myers observed that once Putin had completed his initial training in the KGB, he had

> abundant time to career around the city in the car his mother had given him and, according to his friends, he continued to involve himself in street fights, despite the risk such indiscretions could cause his career. He was indifferent to risk and

danger... in part because his KGB service provided him some protection from the ordinary police. He bent the rules because he could.

(p. 27)

In a later passage, Myers conveyed that "Putin had gotten into a fight during a confrontation on the Metro with a group of hooligans. This time he suffered as much as those he confronted, breaking his arm in the fight. Indeed, he was reprimanded..." (p. 35).

Short concluded that "respect was fundamental for Putin. Whether for himself as a boy in Baskov Lane or for Russia as a great power, the need to be respected was a constant principle all his life" (p. 190). One can guess that respect, the willingness to fight and see it through, and safety were deeply entwined with one another.

Gleb Pavlovsky, who had witnessed Putin's reaction to the apartment bombings[1] in 1999, reported:

> for the first few days after the apartment bombings, there was a mood of utter prostration. No one know what to do... Then Putin said to us, 'you do as you like. I am going to fight. If I lose, I lose. But I am going to make war...

Pavlovsky remembered:

> The day he took that position – he simply felt that this was his moment and this was what he had to do... We had hoped that he would distance himself from all that. Because, without exception, all the politicians who have taken on Chechen wars have bitten the dust. It's a cemetery, a political graveyard. No one comes out of a Chechen war looking good.

(pp. 281–282)

For me, Pavlovsky's comments underscored Putin's compulsion to fight. The context, however, is quite complicated. All of the biographers that I read, with the exception of Short, reached the conclusion that the bombings had been orchestrated by the FSB (the Russian security service) as a means of drawing the country together and creating support for Putin in the upcoming presidential elections – all as part of a carefully orchestrated succession plan that would create receptivity to Putin's leadership after Yeltsin stepped down. We are left wondering, then, whether Putin's comments about making war accurately reflected his state of mind or whether they represented contrivance he relied upon to create political advantage for him. In an adjacent passage in Short's book, Short conveyed that Putin felt the previous agreement Yeltsin had signed to end the first Chechen war had been a mistake. "We've looked on helplessly for too long," Putin said. "We should not whimper and whine... We must stamp out the vermin. If we do not do it today, it will be worse tomorrow," characterizing those who had created the previous agreement as cowards. As Putin considered that the Chechens had created a criminal economy in the republic after the agreement was signed, he asked, "What did Russia do? Nothing... That was sheer defeatism... If you begin to retreat, it leads to more aggression and the number of victims goes up and up" (pp. 281 and 282). Contrivance or not, one felt one was hearing Putin confirm his reliance on combat as a means of consolidating authority and power for himself.

Comments that he made about the "bandit" attacks in Dagestan that occurred in close conjunction with the so-called terrorist bombings suggested that other issues were also at play for Putin: "If we don't put an immediate end to this, Russia will cease to exist. It was a question of preventing the collapse of the country..." These comments presented themselves in Putin's own book, *"First Person"* (p. 140). Fighting, then, was intended to protect one against identity dissolution, a core existential threat that had to be addressed at all costs. State and personal identity appeared to be confounded. A few pages later in his book, Putin extended his thesis:

> They built up their forces and then attacked the neighbouring territory. Why? In order to defend the independence of Chechnya? Of course not. In order to seize additional territories. They would've swallowed up Dagestan, and that would have been the beginning of the end. The entire Caucasus would have followed – Dagestan, Ingushetia, and then up along the Volga River to Baskortostan, and Tartarstan, reaching deep into the country.
>
> (p. 142)

This theme was reiterated much later in the 2011 elections in a pro-Putin video

> that imagined what Russia would be like without him. There would be famine and Civil War and the country would disintegrate, it warned. China would invade the Russian Far East. Japanese peacekeepers would land at Vladivostok, NATO would take over the Western Badlands, and an Islamic emirate would be proclaimed in the Caucasus...
>
> (Short, 2022, p. 536)

A similar reference to existential threat emerged when Putin weighed the compromise NATO had created for Russia. Short described Putin's conversation with an American scholar about this subject: "Our biggest mistake was to trust you too much. Your mistake was to take that trust as weakness and abuse it." Putin purportedly went on to explain that if a bear stops defending its territory,

> someone will always try to chain them up. As soon as he is chained, they will tear out his teeth and claws... When that happens,... they will take over his territory... And then, perhaps they will stuff him... We must decide whether we want to keep going and fight... Or do we want our skin to hang on the wall?
>
> (p. 609)

Myers understood that Putin believed initiating war in Chechnya could well cost him his political career. Putin was said to recall "being a tiny kid in the courtyard who the bullies were 'sure was going to get his butt kicked.'" "Not this time," Myers wrote, "in the Caucasus he was going to 'bang the hell out of those bandits'" (p. 153).

Masha Gessen described Putin's televised appraisal of the war to be conducted against Chechnya: "We will hunt them down, wherever we find them, we will destroy them. Even if we find them in the toilet. We will rub them out in the outhouse." Gessen reflected that

> Putin was using rhetoric markedly different from Yeltsin's. He was not promising to bring the terrorists to justice. Nor was he expressing compassion for the hundreds of victims of the explosions. This was the language of a leader who was planning to rule with his fist. These sorts of overstatements, often spiced with below the belt humour, would become Putin's signature oratorical device. His popularity began to soar.
>
> (p. 27)

Following the elections in 2011, Putin used a "fighting" metaphor to consolidate support for himself in the face of opposition protests. He likened American interference with Russia to the Napoleonic invasion 200 years earlier, commenting

> We will not let anybody interfere in our domestic affairs (claiming that the election process had been distorted by foreign interference). We will not let anyone impose their will on us. We are nation of winners, it's in our genetic code.
>
> (Short, 2022, p. 536)

In an adjacent passage, Short asserted that

> in domestic, as in foreign-policy, Putin had concluded there was nothing to be gained by trying to accommodate his opponents. It was what he had told his teacher, Vera Gurevich, as a boy in primary school, when he was reprimanded for getting into a fight: 'there are people who can't or won't understand, no matter how you try to explain to them. The only thing they understand is strength.'
>
> (p. 538)

In speaking of the hostage taking that had unfolded at a school in Beslan on September 1, 2004, Putin maintained that the country had grown lax and lazy in the face of an external terrorist threat and vowed to take every possible measure to strengthen the state (see Myers, 2016). He conveyed that he believed that "those who had attacked the school had help from nations determined to punish Russia, to keep it weak and pliant" (p. 260). He added that "We demonstrated weakness and the weak are beaten" (p. 260). Earlier he had explained:

> Some (referring to unnamed external sources) want to tear off of us a juicy piece of the pie, others help them do it. They help because they think that Russia as

one of the greatest nuclear powers in the world is still a threat, and this threat has to be eliminated. And terrorism is only an instrument to achieve these goals. (p. 260)

Setting aside, for the moment, the question of whether the FSB had itself played a part in this terrorist act (Masha Gessen made a very credible case that it had), one hears Putin again resorting to fighting as a means of protecting oneself against weakness and incipient invasion – or perhaps it would be more accurate to suggest that Putin's own untethered rapacities helped generate an expectation that others could be as ruthless and as entitled as he was unless he neutered them.

Myers wrote that

Putin brushed aside misgivings about the brutality of the (Chechen) war, saying it was the country's duty to crush the 'brazen and impudent' rebels at all costs… We will not tolerate any humiliation to the national pride of Russians or any threat to the integrity of the country.

(p. 169)

In the face of Western outrage at the systematic destruction of Aleppo in Syria and other insurgent held cities, Putin defended Russian ruthlessness, Short reported, saying, "Look at Israel's example. Israel never steps back but fights to the end and that is how it survives. There is no alternative. We need to fight. If we keep retreating, we will always lose" (p. 590).

On August 12, 2008, Putin attended a meeting with French President Nicolas Sarkozy who hoped to arrange a cease-fire between Russia and Georgia. Myers characterized Putin's behaviour at this meeting as "bombastic and crude, seething with a ferocity towards (the Georgian president) Saakashvilli," whose political sensibilities leaned towards Western democracies. Putin purportedly said that he was going to hang the Georgian president by the balls, justifying himself by telling Sarkozy, "the Americans hanged Saddam Hussein" (p. 352). Fighting, it seemed, was not just a defence intended to create safety for oneself; it was informed by envy and by an intense desire to destroy the other, to obliterate them.

I think the preceding passages tell a story – a trauma story. A story about the impact that Putin's early environment at the Baskov Lane courtyard in St. Petersburg had upon him. An environment fraught with the risk of physical and psychological annihilation for a young boy who was small in stature. While Putin doesn't acknowledge this himself, it's not hard to imagine, as Myers did, that he must have been bullied and that the bullying as well as the ambience of the courtyard must have been quite terrifying for him – young men disinhibited by alcohol, making their way in a poverty-stricken neighbourhood that offered them only limited opportunity for the future, creating status and safety for themselves by affirming their toughness and using it to create a place in the pack. Membership in and acceptance by the pack would have been the primary means that one survived a remarkably threatening, unpredictable environment driven by impulsivity and rutting displays that could be felt, at any moment, to create lethal compromise. Hair trigger potentiality for combat would have only been magnified by the underlying despair – probably poorly articulated – that the occupants felt about their own lives. A version of hyper-masculinity – if one could somehow effect it – would have been the only way out, the only way one could protect oneself. But how does one manage that when one is painfully small and slight of build and when one is suffocatingly scared all the time? For a vulnerable boy like Putin – indeed, for many of the occupants of the courtyard – that world would have been searingly frightening, potentially presenting new threats unexpectedly moment by moment. Even the boys who enjoyed acceptance by the pack would have been hypervigilant; those on the outside of the group would have felt nearly immobilized by it. From a psychologist's perspective, such an environment would be profoundly damaging for many of the people in that courtyard, as, indeed, it seems to have been, as witness the high proportion of criminals that it produced. "Jungle" is not too strong or dramatic a word to characterize the courtyard experience. Bullying, which we now understand is profoundly destructive, would have been endemic. It's not hard, if one gives oneself the opportunity, to grasp what it would have felt like to be in that place relentless day after relentless day.

I do feel, however, that Putin could not be relied upon to provide an accurate portrait of just how suffocatingly scary or humiliating the courtyard would have felt for him; making that admission exposes vulnerability that he would find intolerable. It also potentially elicits a flood of unendurably painful memories that would be hard to accommodate within the context of the strength and the willingness to fight that he has learned to project in order to make himself feel safe. Contriving and maintaining an indelible and unbreachable façade of hyper-masculinity and toughness would feel, subjectively, like it was necessary for survival.

His challenges may have been further exacerbated by a father whose presence was said to intimidate others, by a mother who was said to have cosseted him and possibly overindulged him, and by a family environment in which there was apparently not much demonstrable affection (see multiple sources in Putin's book *First Person* as well as extended descriptions of Putin's family experience in both Myers and Short). Putin himself describes much of his difficult behaviour at school as being a consequence of rebellion against his father (see Myers, 2016, p. 16). There were also descriptions of his family experience that suggested the family was caring, but one wonders how well-equipped the family would have been to have understood the psychological implications of what Putin was facing in the courtyard environment as a small child and a teenager. Both parents had endured literal horrors in the Second World War that had unfolded in the nightmarish Leningrad theatre of operations. In reaction, they, like many of their contemporaries, would in all likelihood have learned to engage dissociation extensively, a kind of emotional numbing, meant to protect one against the intense pain that repeated trauma occasions. Dissociation, particularly when it becomes a habit of being, comes with significant costs: it's hard for people to weigh their own pain and appreciate it and equally hard for them to appreciate the pain that others are experiencing, including their own children. Stoicism becomes elevated as a virtue, possibly culture-wide. Instead of being able to talk about pain, people resort to other means to deal with it, such as substance abuse. As an aside, one wonders whether the high levels of alcohol abuse in Russia are at least in part a reflection of dissociation's impact. The real point in making these comments, however, is to suggest that Putin's parents may not have been very well-equipped to be sensitive to the level of threat that he was enduring. I'm guessing – and it is a guess – that he would have been on his own to handle these challenges.

One also found oneself wondering whether father's intimidating, seemingly cold presence might not have contributed to Putin's compulsive, counter-phobic tough guy stance, amplifying the impact that the courtyard had upon him. It would have been helpful, of course, to have more information about Putin's formative experiences in the family, but the information that is available is too sketchy to allow one penetrating insight. One could speculate that other, unspecified psychodynamics in the family beyond those I have mentioned may have set Putin up to deal with the threat that he experienced in the courtyard by adopting a hyper-aggressive stance, but I don't feel comfortable in providing more elaboration. Other clinicians, however, may see possibilities in the material I provided that they can articulate better than I. Being able to elucidate such dynamics is of course of profound interest and importance.

So how did he do it? How did he manage to transcend his fear-drenched environment and come out on top? All of the sources that I read, including Putin's own comments about himself, emphasized that he has always had high risk tolerance – meaning, one gathered, that he was somehow inured to the effects of fear that would otherwise unsettle or disorganize other people, prompting them to demure where he advanced. Elevated risk tolerance and diminished capacity for fear are extensively referenced in the literature on psychopathy (see multiple sources in Christopher Patrick's "Handbook of Psychopathy"); such characteristics are often seen to be congenital givens, but I wonder if they might not arise as a consequence of extensive exposure to threat and chronic elicitation of dissociation. However that might be, Putin's elevated risk tolerance probably facilitated what he referred to as his pugnacious nature; so, too, would the necessity of negating empathy and compassion in order to engage in the ruthless, brutal, no holds barred style of fighting that initially characterized him. I argued in my book that in my practice I see that people routinely turn off empathy in the face of significant threats to the self, acting in ways that protect the self even though in so doing one creates harm for others. Markedly diminished capacity for empathy is also a characteristic of psychopathic personalities. Whatever the balance between congenital and trauma forces might be in Putin's case, the capacity not to feel would have potentially served him well, making it easier for him to fight back in a remarkably unconstrained manner – one that suggested he experienced little or no regard for his opponent, only desperation to protect the self no matter what the damage to the other might be. In this way, he could create belonging and respect for himself, but at a cost to the humanity that might otherwise have been nurtured in a more benign set of circumstances. Effectively shuttering empathy and compassion would have enabled adoption of a hyper-masculine posture as would low fear tolerance, but in the process, one learns to consolidate a habit of being that profoundly impacts the kind of person that one becomes. Always ready to fight; always ready to push back; always on guard, assessing the other guy's aggressive intent; and always hungry to somehow be the guy on top, the bigger, badder, tougher guy who can overpower the people around him. His toughness and ruthlessness meant he got to be King of the Courtyard; judo consolidated those gains. Becoming part of the KGB meant that he was a member of the toughest "gang" in the country, one that elicited fear in others. It was also a hierarchical structure, much like the courtyard, that he had learned to accommodate himself to and that he had come to develop a visceral appreciation of. Hierarchical structures, one could guess, signified predictability and safety. You were part of a group, like the boys in the courtyard, who could inflict pain and humiliation rather than being subjected to it. And as you engaged with society, you could not only feel safe and protected, but also powerful and special, consolidating and advancing the grandiosity and omnipotence which your position afforded you – grandiosity and omnipotence, in Putin's case, that his earlier experiences as King of the Courtyard and, perhaps, his position as the central focus of his mother's life had already instigated in him.

Compromised Empathy and Cruelty

I would like now to explore the evidence of Putin's investment in brutality and ruthlessness side-by-side strikingly diminished capacity for empathy.

Many of the foregoing passages that I cited attesting to Putin's propensity to adopt a combative stance towards others will have already served to confirm propensity for brutality and shuttered empathy. I would like to cite several more so that both the pervasiveness and immensity of these two characteristics of Putin's personality can be better understood.

Masha Gessen characterized the Soviet world as "going to hell" in 1990, noting, amongst a long list of problems, that "the Soviet economy, too, was nearing collapse. Shortages of food and everyday products had reached catastrophic proportions." She added that

> if Moscow was still able, albeit barely, to mobilize the resources of the entire huge country to get basic goods onto at least some of its store shelves, then Leningrad, the country's second-largest city, reflected the full extent of the disaster.... In November 1990 the Democratic City Council felt compelled to take the terrifyingly unpopular step of introducing actual ration cards...
>
> (p. 102)

Gessen reported that in May 1991 Marina Salye, who was chairwoman of the Leningrad City Council's committee on food supplies, tried to consummate delivery of food for Leningrad that had, as she understood it, already been successfully negotiated. "Salye went home empty-handed, only half hoping that the 60 tons of meat supposedly bought by the city would actually materialize. It did not..." (p. 105). The meat contract was said to be worth 90 million Deutsch marks. As Salye investigated what had happened to the missing meat, she discovered that in May 1991,

> Soviet prime minister Valentin Pavlov granted a Leningrad company called Kontinent the right to negotiate trade contracts on behalf of the Soviet government.... The meat was delivered – but to Moscow rather than Leningrad. The reason was plain: the future GKchP, of which Pavlov was a leader, was trying to stock Moscow food warehouses in order to flood store shelves once (coup leaders) seized power. The name of the man who had negotiated with the Germans on behalf of Kontinent? Vladimir Putin.
>
> (pp. 118–119)

Putin at the time was head of the Committee for External Relations of the St. Petersburg Mayor's office, with responsibility for promoting international relations and foreign investments. Gessen understood that most of the committee's activities were to be centred on providing foodstuffs to be brought into the city from other countries. The coup had unfolded on August 19, 1991, and was said to have been initiated by a group of hard-liners who wished to usurp power from Gorbachev. Gessen asked:

> What is the story that Putin told himself during the coup? Is there a chance he was the person or one of the people in Sobchak's (the elected mayor of Leningrad) inner circle who actively supported the hard-liners? The answer is yes.
>
> (p. 118)

As a result of Marina Salye's investigation of Putin's role in City Hall in the early part of 1992, she discovered that Putin had entered into $100 million worth of contracts with various companies to export natural resources in exchange for food for the people of Leningrad. Salye's "investigation found that every single contract contained a flaw that made it legally invalid: all were missing seals or signatures or contained major (legal) discrepancies" (p. 121). Apparently, while none of the foodstuffs found their way to Leningrad (as previously noted), all the raw materials specified in the contracts had been exported with no tangible return, save for the inordinate commissions (25–50%) that the signees enjoyed. Putin was the lawyer who oversaw the contracts. Salye forwarded on her report about the failed $100 million contracts to the City Council which, in turn, resolved to send it on to Mayor Sobchak with the recommendations that the report be submitted to the prosecutor's office and that Sobchak dismiss Putin. "Sobchak ignored the recommendations in the report itself... So Sobchak did not get rid of Putin. Instead he got rid of the City Council" (pp. 123–125).

30   Richard Wood

Why do I think these events provide a telling portrait of Putin's inability to experience empathy and compassion and enact brutality? Remember that Leningrad had endured some 900 days of a devastating German siege in World War II that had been marked by profound food deprivation and starvation which accounted for a substantial portion of the horrific casualties Leningraders suffered (by some accounts, well over 800,000 people). Remember, too, that Putin's own parents had endured these horrors; his mother had been left for dead on a pile of corpses and had improbably survived after being found by a good Samaritan. As previously noted, during the siege his mother lost one of her children, a son, Viktor, who died of diphtheria, possibly secondary to malnutrition. To give one a better sense of the horror that people in Leningrad had lived through, it is apt to mention Philip Short reported that most of the shocking stories of cannibalism in Leningrad turned out to be true once the city's police archives were opened in 2004 (p. 32). It is against this backdrop of unspeakably tragic personal history in his family that Putin seemingly manipulated food supplies and scarce financial resources to ingratiate himself with powerful others and secure their favour. Catastrophic shortages of food supplies in Leningrad should have been deeply disconcerting for Putin, eliciting impassioned efforts to relieve the people in his community; they did not. Listen now to Putin's own description of the events which led to the failed food deliveries which he provided in his book, *First Person*:

> "The scheme began to work. However, some of the firms did not uphold the main condition of the contract – they didn't deliver food from abroad, or at least they didn't import full loads. They reneged on their commitments to the city… No, there wasn't any real investigation. How could there be? There was no criminal offence." Putin went on to explain that: "I think the city didn't do everything it could have done. They should have worked more closely with law enforcement agencies. But it would have been pointless to take the exploiters to court – they would have dissolved immediately and stopped exporting goods. There was essentially nothing to charge them with. Do you remember those days? Front offices appeared all over the place. There were pyramid schemes. Remember the MMM company? We just hadn't expected things to get so far out of hand. You have to understand: we weren't involved in trade. The committee for foreign liaison did not trade in anything itself. It did not make purchases or sales. It was not a foreign trade organization."

(pp. 98–99)

Glaringly absent in Putin's response is any evidence of remorse or of tortured conscience, notwithstanding his background and the extraordinary suffering of the people in his place of origin. What one hears instead is a dispassionate, almost emotionless accounting of events that he asks his listeners to believe he was not in any position to influence.

Putin's attitude towards remorse appears to be almost matter-of-fact and perfunctory:

> I have some rules of my own. One of them is never to regret anything. Over time, I came to the conclusion that this was the right thing to do. As soon as you start regretting and looking back, you start to sour. You always have to think about the future. You always have to look ahead. Of course you have to analyse your past mistakes, but only so that you can learn and correct the course of your life.
>
> *(First Person*, p. 206)

For people deeply and even only marginally connected to their humanity, regret, remorse, and guilt are an inescapable part of their own human stories; for Putin, they can all too easily be pushed aside so long as one casts one's eyes on the horizon – testament, I would say, to his need to mute those parts of himself that might stand in the way of his ability to pursue the prerogatives of power. Power that confers safety and feeds omnipotence.

Weaponizing food and, one might say more broadly, human suffering, is an important theme that has played a defining role in Putin's interface with the world. Consider, now, his biographers' appraisal of his broad strategic aims:

> On September 8, 2015 the German government announced a plan to take a million refugees per year. By no coincidence, Russia began bombing Syria three weeks later.... Russia would bomb Syria to generate refugees, then encourage Europeans to panic. This would help the AfD (the German populist party), and thus make Europe more like Russia.
>
> (Timothy Snyder, 2018, p. 199)

> During the 2017 electoral campaign, Russian-backed social media in Germany portrayed immigration as dangerous, the political establishment as cowardly and mendacious, and the AfD as the saviour of Germany. In the elections of September 2017, the AfD won 13% of the total vote, finishing third overall. This was the first time since the Nazis in 1933 that a far right party had won representation in a German parliament...
>
> (Timothy Snyder, 2018, pp. 201–202)

> "Russia has a hunger plan. Vladimir Putin is preparing to starve much of the developing world as the next stage in his war in Europe," Timothy Snyder, a Yale historian and expert on authoritarianism, tweeted on Saturday, adding that Moscow is "planning to starve Asians and Africans in order to win its war in Europe." The same article in Business Insider which quoted Snyder also noted that "the US has warned that the conflict in Ukraine could make an additional

47 million people food insecure in 2022. Countries in Africa and the Middle East that rely heavily on Ukrainian grain are especially at risk. Together, Russia and Ukraine provide over 40% of Africa's wheat supply."

(Business Insider, June 12, 2022).

Producing fractures of this kind, globally and within Europe, had been one of Putin's aims. As the economic fallout from the conflict mounted, such divisions, he thought, would become more pronounced. How would Europeans react, Russian officials gloated, when faced with sharply higher inflation, shortages of energy and basic foodstuffs? How long would Europe's welcome last if millions of Ukrainian refugees stayed on indefinitely? What would happen if hunger in Africa and the Middle East brought fresh waves of immigrants towards Europe shores?

(Philip Short, 2022, pp. 664–665)

Vladimir Putin has a plan for Europe and for the world, and he is convinced that he is not very far from achieving it. There are two main components to this plan. The first is no less than the Russian world, while the second involves taking the lead in Europe's conservative movement – conservative in the Putinian sense, opposed to homosexuality, atheism, cosmopolitanism, the Internet and any expression of creativity, which is seen as a symptom of disorder.

(Michael Eltchaninoff, 2017, p. 157)

Instead of directly attacking his European neighbours, Putin encourages European populations to rise up against their leaders. He is sending a digital Trojan horse into a whole series of democracies, and encouraging their own citizens to make use of them. Even more cunning than Ulysses, the Russian president appears to have convinced the Trojans to overthrow Priam and sack the city themselves.

(Michael Eltchaninoff, 2017, p. 168)

And, finally, Eltchaninoff cites Putin's warning to the West offered in the spring of 2014: "I've been telling my friends in Europe for years that if you continue like that, without taking into account the mood of the population in your own countries, then nationalism will rise inexorably. And that was what has happened." Putin attributed the rise of populism to permissiveness with regard to immigration and gay rights (Michael Eltchaninoff, 2017, p. 163). In this chilling passage, one can almost hear Putin gloat about the West's blindness to his strategic aims; his admission strikes me as an act of contempt and certainly not an act of caring.

In addition to weaponizing economies, energy, food, immigration, and exporting hate, one read, to cite but a few examples, about surreal levels of murder and assassination (one of Steven Myers' chapters in his biography, indeed, is entitled "Poison"); Putin's commitment to oligarchy, kleptocracy, and wealth inequality; and the brutal, merciless, deliberately terrifying way in which he has conducted war (at the end of the second Chechen war, no building in Grozny was said to be left undamaged). The scope of injury that he means to create is stunning: tearing whole societies and their social fabric part, generating divisiveness and hate on an unimaginable scale, instigating massive economic instability and deprivation, and starving tens of millions of people and displacing them from their homes. Keeping the self safe through endless acts of brutality occasioned by neutered empathy and compassion enhances the hyper-masculine, strongman image that both defines and constrains his identity; it also creates opportunities to dramatically expand the scope of his power – demonstrating, in the process, the restless, insatiable hunger that characterizes his appetites, hunger which is supported by an extraordinary capacity for brutality. Masha Gessen referred to the concept of pleonexia (p. 266) in her book – the unquenchable desire to acquire other people's possessions. Her term might also be expanded to encompass an insatiable desire to acquire dominion and authority over others, no matter what cost others must endure in the process.

Destruction of Voice

The discussion about brutality and power naturally leads me into consideration of another facet of malignant narcissism: profound commitment to the destruction of other people's personhood, subjectivity, and voice. I would argue that someone who makes such an investment has adopted a fundamentally autocratic orientation in his relationship to other people. The discussion which follows below will review the evidence of Putin's attempts to neuter others' selfhood.

Masha Gessen tells us that Putin, through the second decree of his presidency, began to enact measures meant to strengthen military training and funding. She also reported that he began to undertake efforts to silence the media on his second day in office:

> … Police special forces descended on the corporate headquarters of Vladimir Gusinski's Media Most, the company to which my magazine belonged. Scores of men in camouflage, wearing black knit masks with slits for their eyes and armed with short barrel automatic rifles, pushed their way into offices of the newly renovated building at the very centre of Moscow, about a mile from the Kremlin, roughed up some of the staff, and threw piles of paper into cardboard boxes they then loaded onto small trucks.
>
> (p. 155)

A variety of justifications were provided for the raid – justifications which Gessen described as "confused." Gessen stated that the raid was "also unusual in its alleged initiator, whom Media-Most outlets identified as Vladimir Putin. He himself claimed no knowledge of the event…" (p. 155). Gusinski ended up spending three

34   Richard Wood

days in jail, after which "he left the country becoming the first political refugee from Putin's regime – only five weeks after the inauguration" (pp. 161–162). According to Gessen, Gusinski purportedly signed a document ceding the majority share of his company in exchange for personal freedom. Gessen reports that she herself was threatened as she continued to write about matters pertinent to the Gusinski case. She found someone outside her apartment 24 hours a day and her home phone was shut off. She felt like she was going crazy with unidentifiable worry and eventually decided to look for another job.

On May 13, 2000, only six days after his inauguration, Putin signed his first decree and proposed a set of bills, all of them aimed, as he himself stated, at "strengthening vertical power" – i.e., dramatically consolidating power in the office of the president. "The lone voice against these new laws," Gessen said, "belonged to… my old acquaintance Alex Goldfarb," who wrote, in part, that

> the legislation you have proposed will place severe limitations on the independence and civil freedom of tens of thousands of top-level Russian politicians, forcing them to take their bearings from a single person and follow his will. But we have been through this!
>
> (p. 182)

According to Gessen, no one took notice. The clear manifestations of a repressive, authoritarian personality had made themselves clear to any with eyes to see in the very earliest days of the Putin presidency; moreover, such actions were entirely consistent with the hierarchical structures of the KGB and with Putin's conduct first as Sobchek's deputy in St. Petersburg and later as his deputy mayor, confirming, from a psychological perspective, that in spite of any pretensions otherwise, Putin's behaviour and his choices were founded upon a stable, coherent personality structure that was invested in limiting others' prerogatives of voice and action and their personal freedoms.

Things only got worse over the years. Putin's authoritarian grasp of the country progressively escalated; freedom of expression in the media became increasingly limited and then essentially nonexistent; truth and factuality were persistently perverted to serve state ends (sometimes Putin's and sometimes those of the oligarchs who supported him); and opposition voices faced increasingly harsh, punitive action that could include bogus legal action, harassment, beatings, theft of personal wealth, imprisonment, and poisonings, shootings, and proclivity for opponents to fall out of buildings; the judiciary lost its independence and its independent voice, subordinating itself to the state and, ultimately, to Putin; elections were rigged and opposition parties gutted and/or neutered; and the democratic constitution was eventually replaced by what Putin referred to as a dictatorship of the law. Many perpetrators of these acts of repression in Putin's inner circle received pro forma condemnation or even shaming, but soon found themselves back within the authoritarian fold where they were expected to twin their interests with those of the president. Putin was, indeed, the first person and, one might

Does the Model Fit Putin? 35

add, the only person, capturing the deep irony of the title of his own book. By the end of her tenure in Russia, Gessen commented that:

> I have been saying that working as a journalist in Russia had become virtually impossible: my colleagues have been killed, maimed, and threatened; the government worked in mysterious ways, behind closed doors, turning the job of describing Russian politics into guesswork at best; reporting had become dangerous and pointless at the time.
>
> (p. 292)

Gessen quoted Putin's former Libertarian financial advisor, Andrei Illarionov, about the reasons why he thought a very wealthy Russian oligarch, Mikhail Khordorkovsky, had gone to prison:

> He did not go to prison for tax evasion or stealing oil, for God's sake. He went to prison because he was – and remains – an independent human being. Because he refused to bend. Because he remained a free man. This state punishes people for being independent.
>
> (p. 243)

Timothy Snyder appreciated that the only "historian" Putin valued, Ivan Ilyin, was actually a totalitarian philosopher who either ignored or despised individualism, orderly succession, integration of nation states into collaborative units, novelty, truth, and equality. Snyder said of Ilyin that Ilyin believed "we should long for a condition in which we think and feel as one, which means not to think and feel at all. We must cease to exist as individual human beings." Ilyin, he said, believed that "Evil begins where the person begins" (p. 22).

Snyder also conceived of another important way in which voice was compromised:

> If Russians believed that all leaders and all media lied, they would learn to dismiss Western models for themselves. If the citizens of Europe and the United States joined in the general distrust of one another and their institutions, then Europe and America could be expected to disintegrate. Journalists cannot function amid total scepticism; civil societies wane when citizens cannot count on one another; the rule of law depends upon the belief that people will follow law without its being enforced and that enforcement when it comes will be impartial. The very idea of impartiality assumes that there are truths that can be understood regardless of perspective.
>
> (p. 209)

In another passage, Snyder asserted that "Russian authorities maintained that facts were information technologies from the West and to destroy factuality was to destroy the West" (p. 195). He also suggested that in the Russian reality facts and reasoned appraisal had been replaced with emotion-laden imagery meant to be

36 Richard Wood

evocative and to displace thinking. People's capacity to engage in critical thinking and independent thought was being deliberately compromised to sow confusion and create receptivity to the authoritarian other. This particular assault on subjectivity, while insidious and difficult to name for those subjected to it, can be seen to be quite powerful; information is displaced by misinformation that targets fear and prejudice.

Contrivance and Intimacy

Now I would like to move on to another salient characteristic of my model of malignant narcissism, contrivance of humanity, and interpersonal exchange rather than genuine engagement informed by depth of meaning and attachment.

Philip Short reviewed a number of impressions people had gleaned through their interactions with Putin over the years.

> Putin's actions after joining Sobchak in St. Petersberg gave the lie to the claims of his colleagues in Dresden that he had "absolutely no ambition." On the contrary, they demonstrated a ruthless will to prevail, patient and well hidden, coupled with profound mistrust of the motives of those around him.
>
> (p. 131)

> Many of Putin's Russian colleagues, including those who had little time for Sobchak and his administration, regarded him as an impressive operator. Pokrovsky... said that 'he had a keen mind, he settles everything quickly and has a professional grasp of things.' Aleksandr Belyaev, while stating frankly that 'I don't like Mr. Putin,' acknowledged that 'he understands how to cooperate with people, how to use them in his interest.' Even Valerie Pavlov, who when they worked together, found him 'closed and secretive, never giving anything away,' noted that he had quickly brought whole swathes of the administration under his control.
>
> (p. 162)

Barbara Hay, who dealt with Putin extensively in 1991 and 1992 as part of her affiliation with the British consulate, wrote in her diary that

> (he was) slightly built, quiet, he didn't put himself forward... No small talk. Gave nothing away. Not much finesse... Quite businesslike and to the point. Not social: he was purely focused on the business side of his work... He didn't circulate: he didn't work the room. He never appeared to really want to be there: it was a chore. Not even a duty, a chore.
>
> (p. 163)

Sture Stiernlof, the Swedish consul, found Putin to be "quiet and evasive ...But he never entered into a dialogue. He listened but avoided taking a stand... As a lunch

Does the Model Fit Putin? 37

or dinner guest, he sat for the most part silently with an unfathomable little smile on his lips." Short understood that Stiernloff "did not particularly like Putin and found him unpleasant to deal with." The Swedish consul characterized Putin as speaking so quietly that one had to make an effort to hear what he was saying. He believed Putin was

> too calculating to be someone's friend... He is an operator and manipulator who sizes up opportunities, coldly and soberly, and anticipates his own and others' actions well before he makes the first chess move. He is not spontaneous and he is least of all stupid. My experience of him is as a wily and if necessary, a tough operator.
>
> (pp. 164–165)

Short noted that the American consul, Jack Gosnell, disliked Putin, describing him as "a cold fish. Prussian. No sense of humour." The American ambassador Tom Pickering added that "He was totally closed, whatever he was going to say was based on a significant element of distrust" (p. 165).

Short wrote that France Sedelmayer, who was a young Munich businessman, "came away from their first meeting with an equally unfavourable impression." Putin was "like every typical German bureaucrat I'd ever met, a melange of implied power tinged with self-important arrogance" (p. 165). Short thought Sedelmayer had somehow managed to "get beyond (Putin's) unyielding façade," developing "an unusually warm relationship." As he got to know Putin better, Sedelmayer amended his appraisal:

> He was curious and of course, observant... And he was always in control, both of himself and the situation... He projected himself differently to different people. He was chameleonlike. He give them back a mirror image of what he thought they'd like to see. He was... good at eliciting information from other people, but reserved when talking about others... He was not a person who opened up. (He kept) his private life private... He continually kept a wall between people he knew and his family... I can't remember a single occasion when I had the feeling he was telling me anything revealing about his personal past.
>
> (p. 165)

In another exchange, Sedelmayer had explained that Putin was best with small groups, "one on one or one on two or three" (p. 165). Sedelmayer saw him as an individualist, not a team player, who could become flustered when he had to make a speech or receive a large delegation. Short concluded that Putin was shy, though most of his close Russian friends did not see it. His wife, Lyudmila, however, did: "He had to work hard to seem at ease with people" (p. 166).

The German console, Eberhardt von Puttkamer, was said to portray Putin as someone who preferred to talk of practical things, never anything personal. There was "a door that he never opened," Puttkamer recalled. "He is not a man to show his inner being" (Short, 2022, p. 166).

Gessen had concluded that Putin is "a person who executes all his public acts mechanically and reluctantly, projecting both extreme guard and extreme aggression with every step" (p. 151).

Short emphasized that shyness was just one side of Putin, pointing out that Putin had, in many ways, asserted differences from other people while at school, wearing his watch on his right wrist, "playing the daredevil, choosing a different high school from his classmates..." (p. 166). Myers extended this description, saying that Putin "would walk into class and spin in circles. He was highly disruptive in and out of class" (p. 16). He was once rebuked for delinquency by the neighbourhood communist party committee, which threatened to send him to an orphanage. Myers reported that Putin was a wild and reckless driver, having reputedly once hit a man who lurched onto the road. Putin was said to have claimed that the man was trying to commit suicide; in some accounts of this incident, Putin was characterized as having chased the man as he stumbled away (Putin denied this).

Other accounts that Short provided of Putin's early years suggested that Putin "often gave the same impression of coldness" that his father did (p. 47). Short reported that Putin's closest friend, Borisenko, remembered that there had always been an unspoken boundary in the relationship which he knew he should never cross.

> With him, it was always like this, he seemed to be with the rest of us, but he stood a little aside. He would take part in an event, but even though he was taking part in it, he was looking at it from the outside. He had his own point of view and everything.
>
> (p. 48)

Both Short and Myers observed that Putin became increasingly more disciplined at school, particularly after immersing himself in a regimen of sports training. His discipline and assiduous application to studies resulted in an improbable admission to Leningrad University's law school.

Short also suggested that Putin made an effort to set himself apart from his colleagues later in life through his choice of clothes – green suits and two-tone white and tan shoes, a raspberry-coloured blazer (p. 166). Short took note of Putin's gait during his consecration at the Kremlin Palace, describing him as walking with "his right arm hanging stiffly by his side," which Short understood was "an affectation rather than the result of an accident" (p. 166).

In Dresden at the KGB office, Putin was remembered "as possessing a remarkable ability to adapt his personality to the situation and to his superiors, charming them and winning their confidence... But he would also reveal glimpses of individuality and even perilous freethinking" (Myers, 2016, p. 41).

Myers believed that

> Putin wanted to dissociate his career from the KGB's past crimes, from the ruthless crusades against dissidents to the abortive putsch. He told his interviewer that the KGB had become 'a monster' that no longer carried out the 'task for which it was created...' He insisted that his work involved foreign intelligence and that he had no connection to the KGB's internal repression.
>
> (p. 74)

Short felt that

> Putin knew how to fabricate a credible legend. That had been part of his basic KGB training. Putin had also been taught that a legend need not last forever. Once it has served its purpose, it could be discarded and replaced by something else.
>
> (p. 131)

Short concluded that "Putin did not like ideologies. He was pragmatic" (p. 432). In appraising Putin's presentation, Myers said of him that he

> offered everyone something to cling to, a cipher committed both to the past and to the new democracy, both a patriot and a religious believer. And no one knew for sure what he stood for, because he seemed to stand for everything.
>
> (p. 169)

Michael Eltchaninoff confirmed a similar impression:

> On careful examination of Putin's words at the start of the 2000's, it becomes apparent that he wasn't saying the same thing to everyone. To his European friends he quoted Kant and professed Russia's profound Europeaness. Yet when he went to Asia – and during this period he developed a very active diplomatic relationship with the East – it was a different story. In China, for example, in Putin's first weeks as elected president, he condemned the West and its humanitarian policy... Putin knew that by emphasizing this point he would win the approval of the Chinese leadership, which is not tolerant of others taking interest in its internal affairs.... Putin's liberalism, it seems, varies according to longitude and in the Far East dies out altogether.
>
> (p. 40)

Eltchaninoff concluded in a later passage that "Putin practices a fundamentally à la carte brand of imperialism. According to circumstance, he will conjure up nostalgia for the USSR, shared religious principles, the Russian language, a more vague Russianness, or the Eurasia project" (p. 164). Somewhat earlier in his book, he had distilled Putin's contrivances with terrible simplicity: "The philosophical origins of

Putinism, however diverse they may be, all rest on two pillars: the idea of Empire and the justification of war" (p. 131).

In commenting upon the West's difficulty recognizing Putin's authoritarian core, Gessen wrote "everybody could invest this grey, ordinary man with what they wanted to see in him" (p. 22). She believed that

> if anyone in Russia or outside had cared to pay attention, all the clues to the nature of the new regime were there within weeks of Putin's ascent to his temporary throne. But the country was busy electing an imaginary president, and the rest of the Western world would not begin to doubt this choice for years to come.
>
> (p. 154)

In another passage, she wrote that "(Putin) has been able to exercise greater control over what is known about him than almost any other modern politician – certainly more than any Western politician. He has created his own mythology" (p. 46).

Boris Berezovsky, whom Masha Gessen pointed out had helped create Putin, came to a similarly stark conclusion in 2011: "You understand? The Russian regime has no ideology, no party, no politics – it is nothing but the power of a single man" (p. 261).

There seems to be scant evidence of long-standing, close relationships in Putin's life. It did sound as though he was deeply attached to the judo partner that he lost and to his friend Roldugin in his school years. His time in Dresden as a KGB officer may have also immersed him in a network of friendships that were mutually enjoyable. Overall, however, there was a dearth of evidence that his relational world had been defined by rich, close, personal connections that entailed depth of trust and constructive interdependence. On the contrary, one was left with the impression that he had constructed walls or boundaries that rather effectively separated him from meaningful intimacy with others. His collegial relationships seem to be just that: collegial but not notably personal. Moreover, they appeared to be defined by transactional value. So long as people maintained their usefulness to him and/or so long as their presence was necessary to protect or to project power, they remained in his orbit; should they appear to want to either displace him or jeopardize the network of corruption that helped to sustain his authority, they could be discarded and, at that, rather brutally.

Within his professional circle, relationship security appeared to be largely mediated by kompromat rather than trust, kompromat being the compilation of compromising information that he had about each of his corrupt associates. Having corrupt associates means that one could easily piece together extensive files about their corrupt practices that could be used later to instigate legal action against someone you felt to threaten you. If everybody in the room is potentially compromised by such information, the guy that breaks rules is in real trouble; his colleagues aren't likely to come to his rescue, understanding that if they do, they can face terrible consequences themselves. And, within the Putin administration, because the legal system is so malleable, everybody knows that if you do transgress in some way – that is, in a way that offends the president – spurious legal charges can and often are concocted to tie one up in punishing court proceedings and even prison for years on end. Everyone understands the system and understands that Putin is the man they must all depend upon for the largess and power that he bestows upon them. In this kind of context, it is hard to imagine that Putin could develop a warm interchange with others; this context is all about fear and greed, not depth of affection. Contrivance and posturing would be essential skills, just as they had been in the courtyard. Loyalty rather than friendship would be the defining and foundational interpersonal currency.

But what of his closest personal relationships, his marriage and his relationship with his children? Very little is known about the latter and, other than very abbreviated and one would say glowing idealizations of the parent-child relationship, there wasn't much material in the biographies to examine. There was a little more information about his relationship with his wife, but the references were sufficiently sparse that I would also have to describe them as cryptic. Masha Gessen, who understood that his wife had characterized the very early years together as harmonious and joyful also believed that Lyudmila "pointedly refrained from saying anything about their family life after spy school" (p. 63). Short concluded that

> towards Lyudmila, Putin was profoundly inconsiderate. It reached a point where she wondered whether he was doing it deliberately to see how much she would put up with. Yet she stayed with him, always hoping that one day she would persuade him to mend his ways. Only much later did she realize that was never going to happen.
>
> (p. 83)

In another passage, Short added that Putin was

> exceedingly mistrustful. During their first year together, Lyudmila remembered, 'I had the feeling that he was watching me all the time, to see what decision I would make, whether it was correct or not, whether I passed this or that test.'
>
> (p. 83)

For 18 months Putin did not tell Lyudmila that he was in the KGB, often kept her waiting for inordinate amounts of time when they were to get together, and even, she believed, had her followed by a man who initiated advances towards her, which she turned down. When Putin proposed to her after three years, astonishingly Lyudmila could not determine whether he meant to break up with her. His manner and his words were so hard to read that she had no real sense of what his intentions were when he approached her. Presumably, the overall context of their relationship, which should have established his love and his warmth towards her, did not help either.

In *First Person*, Lyudmila suggested that "the first year we were married, we lived in total harmony. There was a continuous sense of joy, as though we were on holiday. Then I got pregnant with our oldest daughter, Masha" (p. 61). Once married, Short thought that Putin's relationship with Lyudmila was erratic, commenting that "like Sobchek, who was famously unfaithful, Putin's eye was prone to wander" (p. 167). In another passage in his biography, Short described German novelist Irene Pietsch's impression of Lyudmila and of her marriage to Putin. She was said to have become Lyudmila's friend during a summer in Germany. Pietsch characterized Lyudmila, according to Short, as "emotional, unpunctual, easily hurt, given to floods of tears and bouts of pessimism where nothing in the world was right, but also an interesting companion and good friend" (p. 203). Pietsch apparently believed that Putin was the dominant partner in the marriage and that Lyudmila lived in his shadow. Pietsch found the relationship a complicated one. She heard Lyudmila idealize her relationship with Putin, describing him as "exactly the right man for me... I cannot imagine a better one. He doesn't drink and he doesn't beat me...." Lyudmila, however, went on to qualify her remarks by saying, "Volodya must have been born under the sign of the vampire. Volodya's eyes were empty" (pp. 203–204). Steven Myers wrote that "as a husband and father (Putin) proved to be something of a chauvinist... When Lyudmila complained (about the marriage), Putin quoted a Russian aphorism: don't praise a woman or else you'll spoil her. He never celebrated their wedding anniversaries" (p. 42). Myers also made reference to a supposed West German foreign intelligence agent who befriended the Putins "and Lyudmila in particular. Lyudmila confided in her that theirs was a stormy marriage, that Vladimir was abusive and a serial womanizer" (p. 43). In *First Person*, Lyudmila seemed to deny, at least indirectly, that there had been abuse, saying, "Volodya has never taken his problems out on me. Never! He has always solved them himself. Also, he won't discuss a problem until he found a solution..." (p. 150). Later in his biography, Myers commented that Putin and Lyudmila:

> were rarely seen being affectionate or even cordial in public. Their appearances together bordered on the uncomfortable and they had become less and less frequent by Putin's second term. Privately, they live together, dine together with their daughters when they were still at home, and rarely quarrel openly, according to Putin's friend Roldugin, but they ceased to be intimate.
>
> (p. 335)

> Myers reported that one of his colleagues believed Putin had married to advance his career.
>
> (p. 33)

Notwithstanding the veneer of civility which Lyudmila attributed to her marriage with Putin that she and he had settled into after their first year of joy and celebration, the overall tenor of the descriptions of their relationship in the biographies suggest a cold, distant marriage that was at least intermittently seen to be stormy, marked by infidelities on his part, and that eventually ended in divorce. The marriage did not seem to be deeply collaborative. Putin did not sound to be any freer to render himself vulnerable with his wife than he was with anybody else, nor does it seem he could allow himself to depend on her not only to solve problems but to help him through difficult moments. He does not appear to have been any better able, it seems, to drop his strongman posture with her than he was with others. One wondered whether distance had first grown in the relationship in response to the introduction of the Putin's first child, but, on balance, one was left with the impression that the walls which pervaded the rest of Putin's relationships had also inevitably imposed themselves on his marriage.

Poignant comments that Steven Myers made towards the end of his book suggested to me that Putin's solipsism and mistrust had deepened over the years, locking him up in a world in which he felt increasingly beset by potential enemies and in which there was less and less real sustenance to be had.

> Putin's personal life still remained a closely guarded secret to all but those who knew him best, a small and discreet circle, one that had been remarkably consistent over the years but also one that was increasingly insular.…Igor Shadklhan, the filmmaker who interviewed him two decades before, recalled meeting Putin the last time at 1 o'clock in the morning, after waiting for hours as a line of officials and executives filed one at a time into Putin's office. Putin no longer had the easy banter that had won Shadkhan over 1991. He tried to tell a joke, but Putin did not laugh.…Shadkhan now described Putin as terribly tired and lonely, rigid in his dogma, distrusting and afraid even of those in his entourage who would 'want revenge as soon as he steps down because many of them are humiliatingly dependent on him.'

> (p. 429)

Myers wrote that Lyudmila Narusova, Sobchak's widow, reflected that Putin "has a good sense of humour – at least he used to," after which she added that a "certain bronzovenye (had) happen(ed)," which Myers explained was the word for "bronzing, which suggests an inflated sense of self-importance, hardening like a monument into something less than human." In another passage, Myers had written, "each step against Russia he now believed to be a cynical, calculated attack against him. His actions betrayed a deep sense of grievance and betrayal…" (p. 474).

Such comments attest to the fusion of personal identity and state identity that had come to characterize Putin. Injury or grievance to one produced injury and grievance in the other. Putin could no longer buffet himself or his judgement against the wounding that he absorbed either as head of state or in his personal life; one could conceivably bleed into the other, cascading errors of judgement and the retribution he could direct towards perceived enemies. An increasingly grandiose view of the self had further contributed to the injuriousness he could bring to bear on matters of state.

An adulatory documentary intended to help celebrate Putin's 60th birthday inadvertently betrayed the same themes. It showed

> (Putin) surrounded constantly by his aides and guards, but no one else. He worked alone. He swam alone. He ate breakfast alone. No one from his family appeared in either film – neither his wife nor his daughters... Nor did any of his friends. His closest companion seemed to be his black Labrador, Koni...
>
> (p. 427)

Too many battles and too many enemies over far too many years. Enemies, I would say, that he had largely created for himself in his efforts to remain King of the Courtyard and King of the Country. Within the framework that I have constructed, ever-diminishing depth of human connection could be expected to occasion greater starvation, ever more implacable mistrust, and deepening envy of a richness of spirit others enjoyed that he could never hope to possess. Occupying a world that is increasingly defined by what he thinks and feels and that shuts down others' input means that Putin will be more prone to extravagant errors of judgement and more prone to undermine his sense of grandiosity and omnipotence with his misappraisals. To my mind, his increasing isolation suggests that he is entering a potentially dangerous phase of his presidency; one in which the cracks in his tough guy façade are likely to occasion increasingly impulsive, ill-considered decision-making that may have catastrophic consequences for everyone. In such circumstances – and I don't think we're there yet – it is conceivable to me that Putin could employ nuclear weapons.

Impulsivity and Recklessness

At this point in the discussion, I would like to turn attention away from orchestration of self towards impulsivity and recklessness.

The model of malignant narcissism that I constructed suggested to me that impulsivity ought to be as prominent a facet of presentation as contrivance. I don't think that it would be accurate to suggest that Putin's acts of impulsivity stand out as prominently as his efforts to contain and curate himself. Earlier in his life, as a boy and a young man, they did emerge in clear relief through his fighting and erratic classroom behaviour. Later in life, impulsivity appears to be most evident in some of his verbal outbursts, some of which have been described in preceding passages. Masha Gessen alludes to what she calls Putin's "vulgarisms," crude, visceral verbal outbursts in which he directs derision and contempt towards an offending or hated other (p. 265). In those moments – at least on the face of it – Putin appears to drop his formidable reserve and expose underlying primal emotion. A kind of window into the darkness in his soul that he manages to keep firmly shut most of the time. I'm not entirely sure, though, that what we're seeing is as authentic as it seems. I do have the sense that in some instances in which "vulgarisms" present themselves, we are getting a look at the maelstrom under the surface; in others, however, I think we're witnessing tactical manoeuvres that are calculated to shock and to disorganize an opponent or, alternatively, to present a show of force more intended to impression manage public opinion than being a manifestation of genuine antipathy. And that is the problem of attempting to disentangle the meanings that drive Putin's behaviour. In any given instance, it's often hard to be entirely sure how "real" a given behaviour is.

It may well be that impulsive acts and impulsive decisions surface with great regularity in Putin's day-by-day interchanges with staff that we are not privy to, but I could not find clear evidence in the biographies that this is what his staff relationships are like. In his management of the war in Ukraine, one hears repeatedly about generals being fired and being replaced, but one doesn't really know what that process looked like or how it unfolded. It certainly implies but does not confirm impulsivity. So, too, does the great number of Putin critics who encounter various forms of untimely endings to their lives. The overriding impression that I have is that Putin is terrifically calculated and calculating in his interchange with others. He does not demonstrate the measure of impulsivity, so far as I can see, that my model would have predicted of him.

Projective Identification, Splitting, and Blame Shifting

Putin has employed projective identification, blame shifting, and splitting, as perhaps now will be clear through the many examples which the preceding sections of this chapter have provided. The discussion of contrivance and impulsivity will play a particularly important part in establishing an overall framework or context in which to consider these three core defensive operations.

Putin's reliance on contrivance renders it even more challenging to sort through whether projective identification and splitting have unfolded on a largely unconscious basis or are, instead, deliberate tactical manoeuvres intended to serve some transactional end, i.e., consolidation of power, justification for rapacity, deflection from other issues, and instigation of fear and threat, which I have previously indicated I would classify as blame shifting. The biographical record is rife with examples of Putin accusing others of being rapacious, brutal, voraciously greedy, duplicitous, murderous, and grasping when it's clear that these are primarily his motivations, not theirs. Think of his allusion to the stuffed bear, his comments about election interference, his suggestion that Chechnya meant to greedily consume big chunks of Russian territory for itself, and his assertion the school attack at Beslan betrayed unnamed foreign aggressors' attempts to tear off a juicy piece of Russia for themselves.

Such behaviour stands out in particular relief in his relationship with the vestiges of Free Press in Russia that continued to try to express itself before virtually being silenced or, for example, in the attributions he has directed towards candidates competing against him in elections. A small sampling of examples may suffice. After a bruising experience talking to the press about the sinking of Russia's most advanced nuclear submarine, Myers reported that Putin said: "Television? They're

46   Richard Wood

lying! Lying! Lying! There are people in television who bawl more than anyone today and who, over the past 10 years, have destroyed that same Army and Navy where people are dying today" (p. 201). Myers also recounted Putin's reaction to a young female reporter who exposed Putin's flirtatiousness at a shared lunch, hardening "his opinion of the media and reporters who were in his view little more than vultures who sought to exploit or embarrass officials for personal gain" (p. 127). One of the opposition candidates in the March 26, 2000, presidential election, Grigory Yavlinsky, faced

> a late barrage of campaign ads and news reports attacking him as a candidate supported by Jews, gays, and foreigners. The attack, appealing to the lowest common denominator of Russian popular sentiment, reflected a fear that Yavlinsky would draw enough of the country's liberals out of Putin's column to force them into a runoff.
>
> (Myers, p. 184)

In the first two examples, Putin attributes his own mendacity (Kursk) and his attempted exploitation (the female reporter) to the people he sees as having thwarted or embarrassed him. In the third, more complex example, Putin invites the electorate to displace their hatreds and bigotries onto a candidate whom Putin experiences as compromising him, reflecting, presumably, his entitlement to turn contempt and depreciation towards anyone who would oppose him. Implicit in his characterization of his opponent is the intimation that whatever unattractive traits or attributes he understands the Russian population might assign people who are Jewish, gay, and foreign, he does not possess himself. Through negation of the other he invites people to invest in an idealized version of who he is. In the process, he both disguises his own malign intent and acts it out.

The distinction between his ascriptions and the realities that define others again become blurry in his combat with oligarchs who are felt to encroach on his prerogatives. One might say that he knows full well that they embody the accusations he directs towards them, as he knows he does himself, but in making accusations and in assuming a posture of moral indignation he draws attention away from his own acquisitiveness or corruption or brutality. The acts of splitting that he undertakes as he targets various groups like homosexuals in Russia and "Nazis" in the Ukraine, designating them as enemies who need to be expunged to protect mother Russia, also strike one as sheer contrivance on his part meant to serve some important political end, much like the ascriptions he directed towards Yavlinsky. Well aware that a majority of Russians oppose homosexuality, he conflates it with pedophilia and with Western liberal conspiracies meant to tear apart the social fabric of Russian society. Invocation of Naziism, which he conflates with Ukraine's Jewish president, is an equally improbable – if not outrageous – undertaking. The first permits him to create an external threat around which Russians can unite as he cynically manipulates prejudice about homosexuality and the second offers him opportunity to generate justification for a war of aggression and territorial expansion. In both instances, he gets to portray himself as a righteous saviour deeply committed to looking after the best interests of the governed when, in fact, he is ruthlessly self-interested. None of these "manoeuvres" looks primarily like an unconscious defence meant to safeguard the self against its most unattractive impulses by projecting them onto and into others (classic projective identification and splitting); rather, they impress one as manipulation born of an absence of compassion and, I would say, as a repetition of a tenacious and powerful trauma dynamic. Living in a projected world in which one expects others to be as malevolent as one is oneself makes the world a very dangerous place. You have to take out, neuter, or control the enemies around you before they can impose themselves on you, much as he had to do in the courtyard and later in the insular, paranoid world of the KGB that he all too readily accommodated himself to. The difficulty as one surveys Putin's behaviours, of course, is discerning – or disentangling – the variety of motivations that shape his actions. In any given instance, it is conceivable to me that when one sees what looks like projective identification and splitting, one is seeing multiple layers of both conscious and unconscious intention. Such a view is consistent with the way I have framed malignant narcissism.

Also consistent is an expectation that as injurious acts directed towards others multiply over a course of a lifetime and as one's internal world becomes increasingly defined by ugly, blighted imagery, a profound sense that one is monstrous – essentially unable to love and give or engage in generativity – becomes more prominent. The malignant narcissist's damaged humanity becomes a terrible secret that he must find a way to hide from others' view. He does this by calling attention to his aggrandized self, the self that he would ask others to believe is possessed of larger-than-life talent, acumen, and competence which he invites others to identify with and borrow from him. Look over here; don't look at the hole in my soul; celebrate my greatness and bask in the reflected glory of my power. This whole operation contributes a quality of precariousness to the narcissist's endeavours, further exacerbating his sense that potential enemies are everywhere. Precarious or not, it is a balancing act that many malignantly narcissistic leaders manage to carry off over very long periods of time.

Notwithstanding the narcissist's remarkable ability to hide his core flaws, I would suggest that under the surface he experiences a growing fear of confronting his actual self, the malignant self. His fear of facing the terrible actualities inside render it imperative to avoid examining the self. Exposure to accountability is unbearable, not only because it threatens omnipotence, but because it presents the narcissist with a mirror he cannot bear looking into. I have suggested that despite his best efforts to avoid the horrifically damaged self, there are inevitably moments of horror at what he sees in the self. My clinical experience tells me that these moments are fleeting and relatively rare, but nonetheless quite poignant when they do occur. Whether Vladimir Putin experiences such moments is beyond my power to know, but I would guess that he does. His unnamed and poorly articulated dread of looking at what he has become argues that projecting the bad parts of self into others must at times be a core defensive operation (again, so-called classic project identification) intended to insulate him against self-awareness.

For Putin, democracy constitutes a fundamental, existential threat; societies which attempt to empower individuality, personal voice, and reason are, by their very nature, subversive to those that are autocratic and repressive. I think Putin genuinely – and probably accurately – experiences democratic societies as enemies who mean to undercut and compromise his authority and his control. Democracy clearly hopes to proliferate itself. That's undeniable. It would be very understandable that he perceives it as a competitor that intends to displace not only him but any other nations dominated by strongmen. It makes sense that he would attempt to consolidate alliance with other strongmen and that any alliance he established with democratic nations would be only veneer thin, marked by deep mistrust and mutual attempts to deconstruct each other.

The question for me is how deeply and compellingly he experiences this antipathy. Does he appraise the differences between democracy and autocracy dispassionately, or do these differences become intensely, personally, emotionally compelling for him? My own appreciation is that as fusion of personal and national identity further consolidates itself, Putin's reactions to perceived Western encroachment would be expected to be experienced on an increasingly vindictive, visceral level, further enveloping him in a hostile, combative posture in which his opponents are regarded as being possessed of malevolent intent. Subjectively, Putin becomes the cornered rat he warns us about in his book, *First Person* – prepared to defend his territory and his prerogatives at virtually any cost, much, one would think, as he had to as a child in the courtyard. As I said earlier in the chapter, I don't think we're there yet, but as he isolates himself further from meaningful human connection and from the possibility of effective collaboration, these dangers grow. His own desperation and ruthless will to survive feels more and more like that's what he imagines his adversaries – both inside Russia and outside the country – are feeling towards him. So while his warning may have been disingenuous when it was offered at the turn-of-the-century (Putin would have us believe that he would never corner anyone himself), I think increasingly it captures who he is becoming. For me, this is the essence of Putin's brand of projective identification: he increasingly experiences others as being as combative, as ruthless, and as cornered as he feels himself to be. His perception means that he is capable of attacking pre-emptively because he imagines that others would do as he does. It also means that his poorly understood fright catapults him into engaging in provocation and threat that elicits similar response from those people he perceives to represent threat for him, often invoking counter-responses that mirror his own. It appears to me that he is inevitably moving from contrivance, unquenchable ambition, and ruthlessness towards a particularly toxic and destructive paranoid position that will dominate his decision-making.

War represents the most lethal and destructive manifestation of projective identification. Enemies are imbued with simplistic, brutal characterizations reflective of that which an adversary finds most unattractive in others and in themselves.

Now the derogated group can be justifiably attacked and subjected to unspeakable rapacity. In the process, the targeted group inevitably begins to act out cruelty of its own, confirming, in many ways, the worst expectations their adversary has assigned them – a bloody pattern leaving its imprint on human affairs reiterating itself endlessly that no one seems to have been able to stop.

Putin's brand of warfare is both physical (Ukraine, Chechnya, Georgia) and subversive, weaponizing immigrants, energy, food, and economic and political instability. The costs from the latter may be far greater than the costs from the former and certainly just as deadly. All warfare is characterized by both physical and subversive acts; what concerns one about Putin is the alarming scope and breadth of the subversive acts that he hopes to consummate, using a relatively limited military action and the pressures it generates to deconstruct the liberal democracies around him. In the process, he moves humanity towards a darker version of itself.

Inner Life

The final facet of my model of malignant narcissism that I would like to discuss is the narcissist's blighted, devastated interior. The most effective means of appreciating what Putin's inner life might look like is a successful treatment relationship, one in which he feels safe enough to take extraordinary risks with himself and allow others to understand his torment. But, as one can see through the discussion which has just unfolded, it is very unlikely that he would choose to do so. Doing so would necessitate compromising foundational defensive structures. As an alternative, one can turn towards an examination of the worlds that he constructs for himself and for the people around him to live in. I am arguing that these worlds must, upon close examination, yield a portrait of what the inner one looks like. I am suggesting that in important respects, the world of relationships that we build for ourselves finds its foundations in the prominent internal realities that pervade the intrapsychic realm. That is not to say that larger social forces don't make a formidable contribution in shaping our inner space. They do of course. My argument is that, however, inner life comes to assume the shape or form that it does, it manifests itself in our interface with the world.

Consider this very powerful passage extracted from the prologue to Masha Gessen's book:

> … What I found in St. Petersburg was a city – Russia's second-largest city – that was a state within a state. It was a place where the KGB… was all-powerful. Local politicians and journalists believed their phones and offices were tapped and it seemed they were right. It was a place where the murder of major political and business players was a regular occurrence. And it was a place where business deals gone sour could easily land someone behind bars. In other words, it was very much like what Russia would become in a few years, once it came to be ruled by the people who ruled St. Petersburg in the 1990s…. St. Petersburg had preserved and perfected many of the key features of the Soviet state: it was a

system of government that worked to annihilate its enemies – a paranoid, closed system that strove to control everything and to wipe out anything that it could not control.... This was the most frightening story I ever had to write: never before had I been forced to describe a reality so emotionless and cruel, so clear and so merciless, so corrupt and so utterly devoid of remorse.

(pp. 8–9)

A world defined by rampant greed and unfettered appetites. By deep mistrust and profound suspicion. By endless, ruthless combat and competition. By murder. By omnipresence danger and eternal vigilance. By an investment in control that permits one to annihilate an enemy. By an absence of remorse and compassion. By endemic fear and by endemic chaos. By an absence of love. This was the world that Putin occupied, the one that he played such a crucial role in building and the one that he extended to the rest of Russia once he became president. A trauma world, as I have said. The world of the courtyard replicating itself seemingly endlessly. A man who can't trust, who can't feel, who mustn't allow himself to experience remorse or empathy, whose only solace is to be found in the power to acquire more power so that, if needs be, he can annihilate others, and a man who makes himself feel safe by generating threat for the people around him. An internal world populated with images coloured by envy, greed, fear, exploitation, ruthlessness, vengefulness, mistrust, lethality, grandiosity, and power supported by brute force. Where, in the face of such a reckless, unpredictable, dangerous external and internal surround could one find peace, safety, and any of the sustenance that trusting, loving exchanges could provide? Gessen has provided a measure of the man and of the tragic, desolate internal landscape he must endure.

As the reader considers the analysis that I have provided, it is important again to remember that my commentary does not grow out of direct clinical examination but, rather, close scrutiny of biographical data and commentary that some of the people who knew Putin have offered as well as limited autobiographical data. Analysis carried out in this fashion may represent one of the most viable means that we have of investigating dangerous leaders; as Robert Gordon has pointed out in his unpublished work, direct clinical examination of personalities that in particular fall on a psychopathic spectrum is not likely to be effective and could be expected to yield significant misrepresentations of a given individual's life experience. Psychotherapeutic assessment is, by definition, a collaborative endeavour that both patient and therapist willingly make a deep investment in. Such collaboration may be seen to be out of reach in the present instance and even potentially dangerous for the assessor or the therapist. Standardized testing, in turn, is also subject to misrepresentation and personal distortion; such testing may permit identification of efforts to deceive but attempts to construct a portrait of what the actual underlying personality looks like in such instances face real constraint. Forensic psychological assessment provides us with precedent for evaluation of personality based upon verifiable behavioural correlates, as Dr. Gordon will show us. In such a framework, it is important to underscore the limitations of the methodology that one is using, but that is not to say that a forensic format cannot and does not yield meaningful findings.

In the context of grave risk of harm that dangerous leadership can impose, I would maintain that mental health professionals do face an uncomfortable but necessary duty to warn. Failure to do so potentially facilitates unspeakable devastation.

It would appear the biographical and autobiographical data correspond closely in most respects to the expectations of the model of malignant narcissism that I have described in Chapter 1. The one major exception – and it's potentially an important one – is that one does not see the measure of chaotic impulsivity disrupt contrivance and personal presentation to the degree that the model suggests ought to be expected. As previously noted, the continuous parade of Putin critics who have apparently been murdered over the course of his presidency perhaps with escalating frequency could be seen to suggest a rash, reckless, vindictive nature that expresses itself in fits of murderous impulsivity, but one also has to acknowledge that these executions may have unfolded as casual dispensations of death, as Kernberg would say. One would have to witness the emotional state that attended Putin's decision to act lethally in order to confirm ruptures in his contrivance. There are also strong hints that Putin's conduct of the war in Ukraine has been infiltrated by impulsivity, but there is no clear, documented evidence that this has been so, other than inferential evidence occasioned by firings of generals and what appears to be a discordant, fractured tactical execution of the war. In the main, what one sees is a highly contrived and highly orchestrated personality that, while subject to occasional visceral outbursts, is very carefully maintained and directed. The measure of personal control that Putin demonstrates is so effective that in any given instance it's difficult to establish accountability or motivation, though, I would argue, the overall picture is clear enough, as witness the documentation that this chapter provides. The measure of contrivance that Putin is able to exert over his presentation and his ability to be so many different things to so many different people further enhances the threat which he presents.

I look forward to other clinician comments about the issue of impulsivity and recklessness. With further exploration and discussion, it may well be that we discover that the model of malignant narcissism being considered needs to be amended and adjusted, as the evidence just given implies that it should be. At this point, I'm not sure how to offer a path to reconciliation on this issue.

Relying on the model to make sense of Putin's behaviour has helped me appreciate yet another etiology that potentially establishes malignant narcissism: exposure to an environment that levies virtually daily threat of both crushing humiliation and physical assault. In this sense, the model surprised me, demonstrating heuristic value that I hadn't anticipated. This "discovery" underscores the devastation that economic privation, intergenerational trauma, and social upheaval can have upon individual personalities. Every time we tear economic and social fabric with war, with deliberate efforts to starve others, with economic privation, and with terror, we're probably manufacturing more malignantly narcissistic personalities and more citizens likely to be receptive to their leadership, increasing the likelihood of repetitious cycles of tyranny and destructiveness.

Note

1 A series of bombs placed in apartment buildings in different parts of Russia cost hundreds of casualties.

References

Eltchaninoff, M. (2017). *Inside the mind of Vladimir Putin.* London, UK: C. Hurst & Co, Ltd.

Gessen, M. (2014). *The man without a face: The unlikely rise of Vladimir Putin.* New York: Riverhead Books.

Myers, S.L. (2016). *The new tsar: The rise and reign of Vladimir Putin.* New York: Vintage Books.

Patrick, C.J. (Ed.). (2018). *Handbook of psychopathy* (2nd ed.). New York: Guilford Press.

Putin, V. (2000). *First person.* New York: Public Affairs.

Short, P. (2022). *Putin.* New York: Henry Holt and Company.

Snyder, T. (2018). *The road to unfreedom.* New York: Tim Duggan Books.

Vlamis, K. (June 12, 2022). Putin is 'preparing to starve much of the developing world' in order to win Russia's war in Ukraine. Business Insider.

Chapter 3

Incredibly Wealthy, Catastrophically Impoverished (Regarding Humanity, Love, Empathy, Values)

Whatever Happened to You, Vladimir Putin?

Brent Willock

In 2010, Vladimir Vladimirovich Putin invited A-list Hollywood celebrities to Russia for a fundraising event for a children's oncology ward. During a dinner to thank these donors, he mounted the stage, approached the piano, and began playing the song Dominque 'Fats' Waller made so beloved, *Blueberry Hill* (music by Vincent Rose, lyrics by Larry Stock and Al Lewis). The audience enjoyed Putin's performance very much. They smiled warmly, joined hands, and swayed in rhythmic unison to the beautiful beat of that marvelous piece. Putin later shared modestly: "Like an overwhelming majority of people, I can neither sing nor play but I very much like doing it" (Marquardt, 2010).

Currently, some commentators refer to Putin's performance as chilling (Jeffries, 2019). With shifting circumstances, perceptions and judgments often change.

Readers can time travel to attend this interesting historical moment by Googling "Putin Blueberry Hill." Can you view that evening through pre-Ukrainian invasion and post-invasion eyes?

Would it be politically incorrect and/or proof of moral degeneracy to still enjoy that unusual event, now that we 'know' Putin is 'evil'? Was he evil then, concealing his true nature behind a 'mask of sanity' (Cleckley, 1964)? Can one be a cold-blooded psychopath and anything else?

Contemporary Relational Psychoanalysis has paid much attention to normal and pathological dissociative processes that result in multiple self-states, or even multiple selves (ranging from unintegration and compartmentalization to extremely split relational states of being). From this perspective, an individual could conceivably be a malignant narcissist *and* decent, at different times, under different conditions. Diverse identities can be activated and drawn upon as needed. Boundaries between these different personalities, or subpersonalities vary in terms of permeability versus rigid segregation.

> I looked the man in the eye. I found him to be very straightforward and trustworthy. We had a very good dialogue. I was able to get a sense of his soul; a man deeply committed to his country and the best interests of his country,
>
> President George W

DOI: 10.4324/9781003376811-3

Bush reported to the American people and the world (Robberson, 2020). Was Bush merely trying to establish a good working relationship with the Russian leader? Was he deceived? Deluded? Conventional clinical wisdom holds that there is at least a kernel of truth in every delusion. Can there be a *Blueberry Hill* Putin, a Bush Putin, and a malevolent, criminal thug Putin? If so, how does such a divided personality come into being?

Where Might Things Have Begun to Go Wrong?

We do not have much information about Putin's childhood and his formative relationships with his parents. The official account is that he was born in October 1952 in Leningrad (now again St. Petersburg). His parents were among the few to survive the many years' long, brutal assault on their city by the Nazis during World War Two. Before Vladimir's birth, his parents also suffered the traumatic loss of their two sons. They shared a rat-infested apartment with two other families.

According to the U.S. Center for Disease Control and Prevention (2023), *adverse childhood experiences* (ACEs) can have a tremendous impact for those who suffer them regarding future violence, victimization, perpetration, lifelong health, and opportunity. The more ACE factors one has experienced, the more likely one is to encounter more serious physical health, mental health, drug and alcohol, educational, vocational, and socioeconomic consequences.

In all 50 states and the District of Columbia, the two most common ACEs are economic hardship and separation or divorce of a parent or guardian. Beyond those two stressors, abuse of alcohol or drugs, exposure to neighborhood violence, and the occurrence of mental illness are among the most reported adverse childhood experiences in every state. Nationally, one in ten children has experienced three or more ACEs, placing them in a category of especially high risk (Sacks & Murphy, 2018).

ACEs may even impact children before birth, and in the early postpartum period. Infants born to women who experienced four or more childhood adversities when those mothers were children were two to five times more likely to have poor physical and emotional health outcomes by 18 months of age (Madigan et al., 2017).

Writing from the ACE perspective, Stevens (2022) stated that Putin's early life (poverty, neighborhood violence and, as we shall see, possible loss of his mother, etc.) is a stark example of how childhood adversity is the root cause of most social, economic, and mental health issues, as well as violence and chronic disease. In terms of what we now know about intergenerational transmission of trauma, it is likely that he may have 'inherited' from his parents their wartime trauma, personified by Nazis threatening their existence, ravaging their city, killing their friends and family. Struggling to survive, his parents were too absent and traumatized to be optimally attentive to the youngest member of their family.

Stevens pointed out that we have no information about extended family members (grandparents, aunts, uncles, cousins) who could have compensated for Vladimir's parents' suboptimal availability. Kindness and affection did not seem to have been part of child Putin's world.

Even as Putin's experiences of childhood adversity accumulated, some other positive events affected his trajectory. After years of being labeled a troublemaker in school, a sixth-grade teacher helped him realize his potential. He excelled in high school, learned judo to defend himself, earned a law degree, and was selected to join the KGB. The damage had, however, been done, Stevens wrote, producing a machismo man, distrustful and unpredictable, cultivating disinformation to advance his agenda at any cost.

Stevens cited psychologist Alice Miller's essay, *The Ignorance or How We Produce the Evil*:

> Children who are given love, respect, understanding, kindness and warmth will naturally develop different characteristics from those who experience neglect, contempt, violence or abuse and never have anyone they can turn to for kindness and affection. Such absence of trust and love is a common denominator.... All the childhood histories of serial killers and dictators I have examined showed them without exception to have been the victims of extreme cruelty, although they themselves steadfastly denied this.

Lacking childhood love, abused children who go on to lead nations can inflict enormous damage. Hitler, Stalin, and Mao all suffered years of merciless beatings and other unconscionable childhood abuse. They went on to be responsible for the deaths of millions of people. In Mao's case, 35,000,000.

On and after February 24, 2022, the date Putin launched his 'special military operation' in Ukraine, Stevens found the dictator's statements revealing. For example:

> The purpose of this operation is to protect people who, for eight years now, have been facing humiliation and genocide perpetrated by the Kyiv regime. To this end, we will seek to demilitarize and deNazify Ukraine, as well as bring to trial those who perpetrated numerous bloody crimes against civilians, including against citizens of the Russian Federation.

Considering Putin's childhood with parents who had endured the horrific siege of Leningrad, his statements about "deNazifying" Ukraine – a country whose president is Jewish – and defending against genocide, begin to make sense in terms of intergenerational transmission of trauma. In his mind, he feels constantly threatened by Ukrainian "Nazis" and other persecutory objects, perceiving himself as a victim or potential victim. That vulnerability, and his hyperaggressive defense against it, reflects the ongoing, endlessly repetitive nature of trauma that Freud (1920) discussed in terms of a *repetition compulsion* in his book, *Beyond the Pleasure Principle*. Putin must constantly strive to protect himself, recreating the suffering, terror, deprivations, and deaths experienced by his family and community during WWII, defensively reversing the victim-victimizer relationship so that he is now the one inflicting those same traumata on innocent Ukrainian families.

Putin's Mother

"I know more about my father's family than about my mother's." That sentence begins Vladimir Putin's biography, *First Person: An Astonishingly Frank Self-Portrait by Russia's President*, published in early 2000, following his ascendency to the presidency, the product of an extended interview with Putin conducted by three Russian journalists. "I come from an ordinary family," he stated. "I have had a very simple life. Everything is an open book." He only goes into detail about his childhood after he starts school in Leningrad on September 1, 1960, at the age of eight.

By the time that biography was published, Putin's parents had died. Instead of them, it was his teacher from Leningrad, Vera Gurevich, who bore witness to his childhood in that book: "Volodya's parents had a very difficult life. Can you imagine how courageous his mother must have been to give birth at age 41?"

One must be exceedingly careful with respect to believing anything dictators assert. For them, truth is whatever they declare it to be. Putin's story of his origins may be fallacious. He may not have been born in Russia. Like Stalin, he may have entered the world in Georgia, to parents Putin does not acknowledge, giving new meaning to his statement that he knows his father's family much more than his mother's.

According to Wikipedia (2022), a Georgian woman, Vera Nikolaevna Putina (born September 6, 1926) has, since 1999, when she saw Putin become Russia's Prime Minister on television, stated that he is her son (affectionately nicknamed "Vova"). Her claims contrast with Putin's official biography, which states that Putin's parents, Navy serviceman Vladimir Spiridonovich Putin and factory worker Maria Ivanovna Putina (née Shelomova), died before he became president. The Telegraph, a highly respected British newspaper, concluded that while Vera might simply be wrong, or part of a public relations effort, the story "identifies the holes in the known story of Mr. Putin's past." The official narrative is that Putin's parents were already in their forties when he was born (very unusual in that era) which leaves a gap of over ten years since the births of their previous sons, neither of whom survived childhood. Details of the first ten years of Putin's life are scarce in his autobiography, especially when compared with other world leaders.

Vera Putina lives in the village of Metekhi, about 18 kilometers east of Gori, Georgia. She states that Putin's father is a Russian mechanic, Platon Privalov, who impregnated Vera while he was married to another woman. A Vladimir Putin was registered at the Metekhi school in 1959–1960. His stated nationality: Georgian.

Vera married a Georgian soldier, Giorgi Osepahvili. He pressured her to abandon little Putin. In December 1960, she delivered Vova to his grandparents in Russia. She believes the St. Petersburg-based parents referred to in Putin's official biography adopted him from his grandparents.

Vera reports that Russian and Georgian authorities visited her village to pressure her to remain silent. A schoolteacher, who says she taught Putin, stated that she, too, had been threatened. Vera expressed willingness to do DNA tests.

Russian journalist Artyom Borovik's fatal plane crash coincided with the documentary he was making about Putin's childhood that included information about

Vera Putina. Italian journalist Antonio Russo was reportedly also interested in Vera Putina's story before he was murdered. Such deaths are consistent with many reports of how Putin deals with journalists and politicians whom he perceives to be a threat to him.

Dobbert (2015) believes that if there is truth to this secret concerning Putin's birth, and if it had been brought to light earlier, Putin, born 'illegitimately' outside Russia, may never have become President. At the turn of the twenty-first century, Dobbert began searching for the truth, based on interviews with contemporary witnesses, media reports, and video recordings.

Dobbert states that in January 2000, Rustam Daudov, who worked in a top position in the Chechen representative office in Tbilisi, Georgia, began video recording Vera's story. When Vera learned the man she loved, and with whom she had become impregnated, was married, she ended the relationship and moved in with her parents. Vladimir was born on October 7, 1950. She never told Vova his father's name. When he was two years old, Vera travelled thousands of kilometers, to Tashkent, to train in mechanics, leaving her son with his grandparents.

While in Tashkent, Vera met Georgy Osepashvili, a fellow Georgian who was fulfilling his military duty near her dormitory. At the conclusion of her training, she moved with him back to Metekhi, Georgia, where they married. Georgy had nothing against little Putin – at first. Later, the couple fought about him. "He didn't want him to stay with us," Vera says. They were poor and had their own daughter. Georgy also had to support another son. For several years, unrest plagued the family. Georgy's sister took it upon herself to give Vova to a stranger, a major who did not have children. When Vera found her boy, she concluded: "I have to take Vova back to my parents."

Vladimir couldn't stay with his grandparents long because Vera's father was extremely ill. "My parents had to give Vova to foster parents" when he was about nine years old. Since then, she has "always felt guilty, but I had no choice." Vova's foster parents, Vladimir Spiridonovich Putin and Maria Ivanovna Putina, a childless couple, were distant relatives of her parents.

Vera says Vova's adoptive parents moved to Leningrad. They registered Vladimir with authorities and had his birth certificate changed. They made him exactly two years younger, claiming October 7, 1952, as his birthdate. This allowed Vova, who was now officially not quite eight years old, to repeat first grade at his new school in Leningrad, starting on September 1, 1960. Prior to that, he had attended the village school in Georgia for three years, but had not really learned Russian.

Daudov recorded everything Vera said, listening to her for hours. He spoke to several village residents who still have strong memories of Vova. One of his former classmates now heads the small Metekhi school.

Daudov asked Vera for proof of her story. She smiled, shaking her head.

Vova still carries my last name, but he doesn't want to recognize me as his mother. That's the reason people from the KGB came here to my house. They took along all the family photos and admonished me that I was not allowed to tell anyone about him.

58   Brent Willock

Everything about this story was classified information, they insisted.

"Nobody here doubts that Vladimir Putin is my mother's son," Vera's daughter told Daudov. A neighbor who lives a few hundred meters away, Dali Gzirishvili, is roughly Putin's age. When asked about him, she replied that she disagrees with his policies, but then smiled, saying she attended school with him. In the summer, they often played at the river. Fishing, she said, was his favorite activity.

Daudov pitched this story to his contact at the Turkish conglomerate İhlas that owns several television stations and newspapers. If they provided significant coverage, he hoped, Russian media might report this story. Daudov flew to Istanbul to meet Murat Arvas, assistant to İhlas' CEO. They came to an agreement under which Vera's story would be published in the daily newspaper Türkiye. Later, Daudov's film would be broadcast on İhlas' largest TV station.

The day the article was published, a member of the Russian Embassy contacted Türkiye, wanting to know where the newspaper obtained this information. The film's broadcast was halted. When Daudov asked why, he was informed by Murat Arvas that it was because of Blue Stream, the gas pipeline that was supposed to solve Turkey's energy problems. Russia would deliver up to 19 billion cubic meters of natural gas every year to Turkey through that pipeline. The Russians threatened to stop the project if Turkey disseminated any more information 'against Russian interests.'

In October, a colleague at the Chechen representation in Tbilisi, capital of Georgia, told Daudov that he knows an experienced war correspondent from Italy who is conducting research in Chechnya. The reporter, Antonio Russo, was prepared to travel to Georgia to view the video about Vera Putina. On October 15, Russo met Daudov. After two hours, Daudov gave him the video cassettes. Russo thanked him and departed. Early the next morning, Russo's body was found on the side of the road, 35 kilometers east of Tbilisi, with his hands tied. According to the autopsy, he died around 2 a.m. Cause of death: injuries to his lungs resulting from several broken ribs. "He was abducted and then run over by a truck." The video cassettes he had just acquired vanished from his hotel room.

Russo's death was never completely cleared up. Two Italian investigators sent to investigate his murder were directed back to Italy after just two weeks in Georgia. One official involved in the case hinted to an Italian radio station that the Russian secret service may have played a role. Two Georgian police officers who tried to investigate Russo's death also ended up dead. One was said to have committed suicide; the other was poisoned.

At 1:30 a.m., September 7, 2003, police found the body of Rustam Daudov. He died from five shots fired at close range. Next to his body, officers found empty shell casings from a Makarov pistol. "We are convinced it wasn't a robbery. The victim apparently was out for a walk, during which he was shot. It was probably a targeted act. We still don't know anything about a possible motive," a police officer said.

This victim was a Chechen. The assassins had apparently shot the wrong man. The intended victim, the Georgian, Rustam Daudov, was able to flee Georgia. The

Incredibly Wealthy, Catastrophically Impoverished   59

United Nations obtained exit documents for him and his family, making it possible for them to fly off to a new life in Western Europe.

For weeks, Daudov thought about whether he should meet with journalists from *Die Zeit*, a weekly German newspaper of record. His wife was opposed. Ultimately, she acquiesced. She is still afraid for her family's safety, which is why Dobbert did not use Rustam Daudov's real name in his important story.

Daudov believes that, because Vera Putina is Putin's real mother, Putin could not bring himself to simply have her killed. There is no absolute proof, but Daudov poses three questions.

> First, why did the KGB make more than one visit to Vera Putina in Metekhi, as village residents have confirmed? Second, if he's not her son, why did Putin never try to find the man who really is Vera Putina's son? Third, why hasn't the Russian secret service made the results of Vera Putina's DNA test public?

Sam at Tiramillas.com (2022) claims Putin's maternal grandfather sent him to an orphanage, prior to his being adopted. If any of the above claims are true, they would add to the already substantial number of traumatic losses Putin suffered early in life. Each additional Adverse Childhood Event increases the likelihood of highly problematic outcomes.

How Can Anyone Be such a Heartless, Callous Killer?

How could a person, if they have even a drop of decency, bomb hospitals, kindergartens, children's shelters, maternity wards, daycare centers, and apartment buildings, as Putin did, repeatedly, in Ukraine?

In the interest of expanding our inquiry into this extremely disturbing realm, let us move beyond crucial concepts like dissociated self-states and Adverse Childhood Events in an attempt to fathom what might have transpired developmentally, deep down, in Putin's personality structure. For this purpose, I will call upon British Object Relations Theorist, Harry Guntrip (1969). His important ideas can assist us substantially in our efforts to understand this malevolent mystery. (Note: In psychoanalytic parlance, the *object*, as in Object Relations Theory, is the opposite, or complement of the subject. Object relations, therefore, means interpersonal relations, including complicated, unconscious processing of those relationships, often involving defenses designed to protect against developmentally problematic relational experience.)

Guntrip wrote about a premoral phase of development characterizing the first few months of life. His predecessor, British psychoanalyst Melanie Klein, referred to this early stage as the Paranoid-Schizoid Position. (Paranoid means mistrustful, hypervigilant, prone to projection; schizoid means split.) In this era, babies experience the world in emotional terms: life feels either good or bad. In Klein's evocative imagery, infants believe they are either with the 'good breast' or the 'bad

60   Brent Willock

breast.' These two *objects* are completely separate. If the good breast is not present, then one is automatically with the persecutory 'bad breast'. Life is lived in these binary terms.

Babies have no sense that the good breast can be temporarily absent. The concept of not-yet-present-breast does not exist at this time. When the good breast is not available, that void is rapidly filled by the bad breast. The infant has not developed an image of mother that contains both good and bad features – a representation of her that includes both nurturing and frustrating qualities. The infant cannot yet conceive of a caregiver that is sometimes irritatingly unavailable and, also, a generally wonderful, loving being. Split along affective lines, the infant is either with a purely benevolent or malevolent entity.

Only in Klein's later, Depressive Position, do infants begin developing the sense that they have one complicated mama, not two completely opposite mothers. At this point, babies begin feeling guilty about harm they inflict on their mothers, in reality or imagination (e.g., hateful fantasies). Before then, the infant's rage and destructive, annihilatory fantasies feel totally justified. One must obliterate the bad breast to survive.

Only in the Depressive Position, rather than splitting people and world into totally good or bad, do babies become capable of beginning to conceive of a whole person whom they can regard with realistic ambivalence, based on a judicious balance of basic trust and mistrust (Erikson, 1950). In Klein's important contribution to psychoanalysis, the arrival of the Depressive Position, and its gradual ascendancy over the Paranoid-Schizoid Position, is the most important step in human development.

Donald Winnicott, a pediatrician who became a famous psychoanalyst, was initially allied with Klein. Later, he became a key member of the British Object Relations group to which Guntrip belongs. Winnicott came to prefer slightly different, more ordinary, less technical terms than did Klein. He wrote about a pre-ruth stage (roughly equivalent to Klein's Paranoid-Schizoid Position), followed by the Stage of Concern (similar to Klein's Depressive Position). With the arrival of the capacity to be concerned about the feelings and wellbeing of separate others, babies begin to be troubled that their actions, and even their angry feelings/fantasies, may harm and alienate others whom they also love.

Putin seems to have become partially fixated in a pre-Depressive, Paranoid-Schizoid Position, preceding the capacity for Concern. In that less evolved self-state, he does not care much, if at all, for those whom he maims and slaughters. For all intents and purposes, they deserve the aggression he directs at them. Empathy, guilt, and remorse seem absent in this premoral state.

Unlike those who are characterologically more securely consolidated at a mostly higher, neurotic/normal, stage of concern (organized around more evolved defenses, like repression), in certain significant sectors of his personality, Putin seems partially developmentally arrested at a primitive level, centered around defensive splitting and other, associated defensive operations that affect perception of reality, e.g., projection. While to most of the world he looks much like Hitler attacking neighboring states for needed *lebensraum* and resources, Putin regards the Ukrainians, particularly Volodymyr Oleksandrovych Zelenskyy, as Nazis (persecutory objects) who should and must be annihilated. His destructive drive is not diminished by the inconvenient fact than Zelenskyy is Jewish.

Besides being manipulative, spreading lies of war to advance his agenda, Putin may also sometimes be functioning below the level of what Freud called secondary process (rational thought, delay of gratification, reality testing, etc.). In this constricted, more primitive level of cognition, one must simply eliminate the bad breast (the absent mother, i.e., a Ukraine that insists on being separate, independent, having its own interests that are not always completely aligned with baby Putin's desires). The malevolent breast (anything standing in the way of being with the good breast), must be destroyed. All such entities are evil (Nazis).

Schizoid Personality

The *Merriam-Webster Dictionary* (2022) defines schizoid as "having mutually contradictory or antagonistic parts: changing frequently between opposite states." Extending that definition into the psychological realm, they could be describing a personality organized around multiple conflicting or dissociated self-states, as I believe might characterize Putin's situation.

Moving explicitly into psychological territory, that Dictionary states: "of, relating to, or having a personality characterized especially by emotional and social detachment, indifference, and lack of affect." They quote Theodore Millon, an American psychologist, known for his many contributions to the study of personality disorders: "Extreme schizoids seem impervious to all emotion—even anger, depression, and anxiety—not just to joy and pleasure."

When we think of schizoid personality – elegantly described by Fairbairn (1944), Guntrip (1969), McWilliams (2006), and others – we may be inclined to think of gentle people who are uncomfortable with feelings and relationships. This understanding accords with a no doubt politically incorrect joke some colleagues shared with me:

Doctor A: This gentleman works in the post office.
Doctor B: Provisional diagnosis: Schizoid Personality.
Doctor A: He's been working the night shift for years.
Doctor B: Diagnosis confirmed.

In a brief article on Putin, Israeli psychologist Avidan Milevsky (2014) described him with terms like "loner" and "recluse." These descriptors fit the idea of schizoid personality.

When we contemplate psychopathic dictators, we may not initially think of schizoid personality. Guntrip did not write a great deal about these totalitarians. He did, however, made it abundantly clear that he viewed them as profoundly schizoid.

He understood their unfeeling destructiveness in relation to their cognitive, unemotional, detached, schizoid personalities.

Can one diagnostic label encompass such diversity? Rather than focus too much on manifest behavioral expression, in order to benefit from Guntrip's insights, it helps to consider the underlying intrapsychic, relational situation that may serve as common foundation for diverse defensive manifestations. The schizoid mechanism and structure involve Kleinian splitting of the object world into all good and all bad – defensive operations that Otto Kernberg (1975) illuminated in his groundbreaking contributions to the study of narcissistic and borderline personality disorders. He described how the normal early emotional division of object and world into all good and all bad can, subsequently, become an active, defensive splitting designed to segregate these domains lest the bad contaminate and destroy the good, or create terrifying confusion. That splitting operation (think of Putin's 'special military operation' against Ukraine) may make life more simple, understandable, and manageable, but it can cause other serious difficulties.

When infants encounter the bad object (exciting, attractive, unavailable, dismissing, rejecting, neglecting, abusive, frightening), in their efforts to cope and protect themselves, they are inclined to internalize it, Fairbairn wrote, in hopes that in their minds, they can have more control, less helplessness in relation to it. In the real world, having removed the bad object as much as possible, they are left with a tolerable object with whom they can coexist. They can have a relationship with this more endurable object that they need for survival. Often this splitting strategy does not work as well as hoped. It can fuel nightmares (witches, monsters), behavioral disorders, and other symptoms.

Guntrip believed this distressed ego that has retreated significantly from reality into an internal world eventually undergoes one further, final, fatal split. Exhausted by the struggle with internal bad objects, it now wishes to withdraw from all relationships, be they bad, good, internal, or external. Human relations are too frustrating, frightening. They require enormous work, just to survive. These individuals, therefore, long to regress into a relatively objectless state, to an existence preceding significant encounter with bad objects (i.e., a retreat to the womb). If that warm uterine milieu proves elusive, a cold tomb will suffice. Schizoid suicide may become attractive, though dictators (like Putin) strongly prefer homicidal solutions to this life-or-death struggle.

Much as this overwhelmed ego desires regression away from relationships, that longing is also terrifying since it means abandoning the real world, any potentially gratifying relationships, and sanity. Some, therefore, suppress this desire to retreat, replacing it with terror of dying. It can become hard for them to go to sleep, since slumber may symbolize surrendering attachment to reality and sanity as one drifts off into a cozy, eternal, dark, womb-like milieu. These individuals may, therefore, defend against necessary nocturnal relaxation, tensely holding onto some connection with the real world, leading to restless insomniac nights. But one must sleep. Sometimes medications knock them into needed unconsciousness.

Besides characterologically consolidating around their significant fixation point in the pre-Concern stage, totalitarians may manically amplify that desired, pre-ruth orientation into one of *ruthlessness*. Better to terrify and inflict death onto others, to be the deliverer of these intolerable things, than to receive them. Far more desirable to be the bad object than to be its victim. By means of this defensive turnaround, these autocrats no longer feel weak and vulnerable to attack. Others, not they, will tremble and flee from Vladimir the Terrible.

Functions of Delusions

A beloved relative recently asked me if I thought Putin had a breakdown around the time he invaded Ukraine. This lovely young woman knew a thing or two about psychic collapse. Her question was insightful. Who can view recent pictures of Putin at the far end of extremely long tables, talking with some other world leader, such as France's Emmanuel Macron, without thinking the Russian dictator is inhabiting some very strange, perhaps schizoid, paranoid state? In videos of him grilling, sometimes publicly humiliating, important members of his government, he seems profoundly alienated not only from foreign heads of state, but even from those in the inner circle of his regime.

Freud understood paranoid delusions as representing attempts to reconstitute a livable environment after one's psychic world has collapsed. Think of his 1911 discussion of Daniel Paul Schreber, a highly respected German judge, who became floridly psychotic. Schreber is now best known for his delusional memoir that portrayed God wanting to impregnate him in order to begin a new human race. The bad object world would be replaced with a new, good one. To accomplish this desideratum, Schreber knew he had to be gradually transformed into a woman.

Unlike Judge Schreber, Putin would be utterly repulsed by that necessity to be feminized. Vladimir must vigorously assert, even flaunt, masculinity. Rather than submitting to feminization like Schreber, he strongly prefers to castrate or even kill others. In keeping with this vicious defensive need, the Russian president lashed out at a journalist for the prominent French newspaper, *Le Monde,* who irritated him by daring to question Putin's callous, destructive behavior in Chechnya:

> If you want to go all the way and become a Muslim radical and are ready to get circumcised, I invite you to Moscow. We are a multi-confessional country, we have experts in this field, too. I will recommend that they carry out the operation in such a way that nothing grows back.

> (Zolotov, 2002)

Putin's sadistic fantasies of genitally mutilating opponents may be viewed as at least less lethal than his other fondness for having his expert assassins inject journalists, politicians, and others whom he dislikes with deadly substances designed to prevent any life whatsoever from ever growing back.

Putin had his own idiosyncratic way, different from Schreber's, for re-establishing a viable, paranoid, perhaps delusional world where he could feel safely in charge in an omnipotent, God-like manner. Delusions are less extreme, disturbing, and isolating if they are supported by cultural contexts. For example, if an adolescent girl ensconced in Roman Catholic tradition claims she saw and spoke with the Virgin Mary, that is less concerning than if a young woman outside the Catholic faith had the same 'hallucination.' Putin's delusion about Nazis and the genocidal activities they were conducting against Russians in Ukraine fits an earlier time and place (World War Two). As a result, he may not seem totally crazy to everyone. His far-out ideas might appeal to some who are traumatically fixated on that earlier epoch. To them, it might make sense to be grimly determined to eliminate Nazis and genocide wherever one thinks they might be, and to try to recover some of what is felt to have been lost, appropriated unjustly by these persecutory objects.

Where Did You Go, Vladimir?

In schizoid personalities, parts of self continue struggling with external and inner realities, while another significant ego chunk abandons all object relationships, external and internal. This "lost heart of the self" (Guntrip, 1969, p. 87), buried snugly, or chillingly, in some internal womb or tomb, contains "the lost capacity to love" (p. 90). Without conscious, adequate access to this abandoned self, daily life is empty, unfulfilling, and lonely.

Schizoid personalities usually know they do not have the capacity to feel with the emotional warmth and lively interest that others manifest. Having lost so much of their original libidinal selves, they cannot form deep, loving ties. Others cannot easily get in touch with them. Their living hearts have fled the scene, regressed deep within. May all the above have happened to you, Vladimir?

Guntrip's ideas concerning wishes to retreat to the quiescence of womb or tomb might provide an alternative, or complementary explanation to Freud's (1920) speculations concerning a death drive (a hypothesized longing of living organisms to return to an evolutionarily prior, inanimate state). Contemplating these matters from Guntrip's framework, Thanatos would not be a built-in, biological drive but, rather, a common reaction to life's frustrations based on memories of an easier, prenatal time.

When one considers the enormous destruction Putin inflicted on Ukrainians, it is hard not to notice his apparent pleasure and satisfaction in returning so many of them to an inanimate state. He seems to embody a death drive. As discussed earlier, I see this destructiveness as a primitive psychological defense mechanism rather than as the manifestation of an innate biological drive.

In some patients, the wish to die covers a deeper feeling that the vital heart of the self actually did die, in some sense, in early childhood. The sensitive, feeling heart of the infant psyche, having retreated so far within, leaves an empty shell of a person behind to go through the motions of living a life lacking much meaning.

"In the seriously schizoid person, the vital heart of selfhood and the active quest of object-relations are alike paralyzed, resulting in a condition out of which the individual cannot help himself" (Guntrip, 1969, p. 92). With the capacity to love and be loved grossly inhibited, individuals become helpless victims to the regressive pull to passivity and inner deadness. Putin has little or no tolerance for any such passive yearnings. He vigorously rejects any such dangerous longings. He repeatedly demonstrates to himself and the world that he is not passive, not a walking corpse. He is, rather, an extremely active, initiating, controlling, hypermasculine entity. "Feelings of despair, loneliness, weakness, and incapacity to love always lie hidden behind the cold detached mask of the schizoid personality, however stable he may appear to be" (Guntrip, 1969, p. 97).

> When the mother cannot tolerate the infant's demandingness, he becomes afraid of his own love needs as ruthless and destructive... The ego...starved of satisfaction of libidinal needs...experiences an angry urge to hit back aggressively, at the rejective outer world that drove it into retreat.
>
> (Guntrip, 1969, p. 102)

One can imagine Putin moving this original relational struggle into his internal world, then projecting it back onto the external environment, striking back viciously at what he perceives to be an unjustly depriving, persecutory milieu.

Schizoid egos are haunted by a sense of nonentity, emptiness, and feared ego collapse. One way for Putin to fill such a dangerous void might be to identify with something grand, like Mother Russia. His personal lack of developmental continuity could thereby be papered over via grandiose identification with a national destiny that goes way back in time, and far forward. In this delusional symbiotic bliss, Mother Russia and he are one. He is his mother/Mother Russia who endured the horrific siege of Leningrad, then pushed westward to exterminate Nazis in Berlin, next in Kyiv, next in....

> Fear of loss of contact with the external world constantly motivates efforts to regain contact with it, but this cannot be done by loving relationships, and therefore can only be done in terms of the other two emotional reactions, fear and aggression. To relate simply in terms of fear sets up the paranoid state, which can pass over into the cold-blooded defence of mere destructive aggression.
>
> (Guntrip, 1969, p. 101)

Is There Any Hope for the Likes of Putin?

Guntrip's second psychoanalyst (after Fairbairn) was Winnicott (1963). The latter described a state of affairs strikingly similar to Guntrip's concept of the regressed, retreating, schizoid ego. Winnicott's "incommunicado" self is an "isolate" (p. 187). Forever fearing being found, it also, paradoxically, longs to be located. "It is a joy to be hidden, but a disaster not to be found" (1965, p. 186). This conflicted yearning manifests in many criminals (Willock, in preparation).

Part of Putin would long to be reached by others but would be terrified of that possibility. He would avoid and fight that yearning ruthlessly. Dictators are not inclined to seek psychoanalytic therapy which might enable them to re-establish

66   Brent Willock

contact with the lost heart of their selves. For these tyrants, psychotherapy connotes despicable weakness, dependency, femininity, vulnerability, terror of getting in touch with warded-off feelings and relational trauma. Far better to destroy millions of others rather than risk being overwhelmed and annihilated by recontacting repressed horrors. Covering the lost heart of their selves with psychopathic armor, these totalitarians provide for themselves an illusional sense of power, safety, independence, and esteem.

Despite the growing public acceptance and destigmatization of psychotherapy, Putin (and his type) is unlikely to enter treatment, unless he were to completely break down and find himself unable to summon his usual defenses (e.g., attacking nations, assassinating political rivals and journalists who displease him and threaten whatever limited security he may have). He then might find himself hospitalized, exposed to some sort of therapy. In the contemporary zeitgeist, that treatment would likely be limited mostly to drugs intended to make him feel better, rather than involving the human, insight-oriented therapy he would actually need.

Putin stole enormous wealth from his country. Finances would be no obstacle to his obtaining treatment. In the unlikely event that he were ever to engage in psychoanalytic psychotherapy, perhaps he would create a dream like that of Guntrip's patient, a man in his late forties, of marked ability, who carried heavy responsibilities, while feeling grave strain and exhaustion:

> I was living in a dugout. It was covered over completely at the top and there was a mechanical turret at ground level which revolved. It had two periscopes [eyes] which brought me information of what was going on outside, and two slits [ears] through which sounds could come to be recorded on tape for me, and an opening [mouth] through which I could send out messages from my tape recorder.
>
> (p. 105)

This profoundly withdrawn, schizoid imagery – that Heinz Kohut (1977) would classify as a self-state dream – captures Putin's likely intrapsychic situation, though his current isolation chamber is an ornate palace, surrounded by barriers, armed guards, and other formidable security measures (including policies to annihilate unwanted individuals and nations).

A central feature of the Depressive Position is the desire to make *reparations* to the object one believes one has harmed. If Putin were to emerge from his paranoid-schizoid position to allow for a more depressive position, he would have plenty of opportunities to provide much-needed reparations. Justice demands he deliver enormous restitutions to the Ukrainian people.

The deepest element to be reached in psychoanalytic therapy is the patient's experience of the failure, non-possession, or absolute loss of an adequate mother, and fear of re-experiencing that original maternal deprivation, Guntrip wrote. These individuals fear breaking down in an environment devoid of support. Far preferable to weaponize one's self via merger with one's powerful country, then acting out these horrific internal dramas on the global stage, insisting on regaining full possession of mother (Georgia, Chechnya, Ukraine, etc.), transforming primal failure into glorious, horrific success.

Coda

Blueberry Hill's lyrics resonate with the idea that Putin suffers from primal (parental) loss, resulting in what Hungarian/British psychoanalyst Michael Balint (1968) called a *basic fault* in personality structure. Balint (1959) wrote a great deal about thrills and regressions related to this internal fault line. Fats Domino clearly found his thrill on Blueberry Hill. Putin would dearly like to do likewise but, less capable of loving and enduring loss, he must, instead, pursue perverse thrills via invasive conquests of individuals and nations.

Blueberry Hill's songwriters' fondness for music preceded Putin's. These talented individuals penned the lovely idea that the wind in the willow played love's sweet melody. They went on to couple that sweet sentiment with something sad, namely that all those vows someone made were never to be. How can one cope with such disappointment and loss? The songwriters provided one important possible answer. Though we're apart, you're part of me still. Clearly, they have rich internal lives in which lost loves can be memorialized and enjoyed, even though sadness surely and inevitably accompanies such separations.

Dodging acknowledging and dealing with such loss, identified defensively with his version of Mother Russia, Putin continues to be convinced that Ukraine is 'part of him still.' Unlike the songwriters, the dictator acts out this fantasy in a vicious manner. He insists Ukraine is not a real, separate nation. It is part of him/Russia still. He must compel that necessary reunion. It is a matter of life or death. There will be sound, fury, endless suffering, multitudinous deaths. One will not hear any wind in the willow playing love's sweet melody.

References

Balint, M. (1959). *Thrills and Regressions*. New York: International Universities Press.
Balint, M. (1968). *The Basic Fault: Therapeutic Aspects of Regression*. London: Tavistock.
Cleckley, H.M. (1964). *The Mask of Sanity: An Attempt to Clarify Some Issues about the So-Called Psychopathic Personality* (4th ed.). Saint Louis, MO: C.V. Mosby Co.
Dobbert, S. (2015). Vera Putina's lost son. *Zeit Online,* May 7. Translated by Charles Hawley and Daryl Lindsey. Available at https://www.zeit.de/feature/vladimir-putin-mother?utm_referrer=https%3A%2F%2Fwww.google.com%2F, accessed on January 10, 2023.
Erikson, E.H. (1950). *Childhood and Society*. New York: Norton.
Fairbairn, W.R.D. (1944). *Psychoanalytic Studies of the Personality*. London: Tavistock.
Freud, S. (1911). Psycho-Analytic Notes on an Autobiographical Account of a Case of Paranoia (Dementia Paranoides). *The Standard Edition of the Complete Psychological Works of Sigmund Freud*, 12, 1–82.
Freud, S. (1920). Beyond the pleasure principle. *S.E.,* 18.
Guntrip, H. (1969). *Schizoid Phenomena, Object-Relations and the Self*. New York: International Universities Press.

Jeffries, S. (2019). The world according to Putin review—sex, lies and state-approved videotape. *The Guardian,* October 30, 2019. Available at https://www.theguardian.com/tv-and-radio/2019/oct/30/the-world-according-to-putin-review-sex-lies-and-state-approved-videotape, accessed on December 31, 2022.

Kernberg, O.F. (1975). *Borderline Conditions and Pathological Narcissism.* New York: Aronson.

Kohut, H. (1977). *The Restoration of the Self.* New York: International Universities Press.

Madigan, S., Wade, M., Plamondon, A., Maguire, J.L., & Jenkins, J.M. (2017). Maternal adverse childhood experience and infant health: Biomedical and psychosocial risks as intermediary mechanisms. The Journal of Pediatrics, 187, 282–289.

Marquardt, A. (2010). Vladimir Putin: Prime Minister, action man, crooner. *ABC News,* December 13, 2010. Available at https://abcnews.go.com/International/vladimir-putin-sings-blueberry-hill-charity/story?id=12381482, accessed on December 31, 2022.

McWilliams, N. (2006). Some thoughts about schizoid dynamics. *Psychoanalytic Review,* 93(1), 1–24.

Merriam-Webster Dictionary. (2022). Available at https://www.merriam-webster.com/dictionary/schizoid, accessed on January 6, 2023.

Milevsky, A. (2014). Putin's dark sibling psychology and the crisis in Russia. *Psychology Today,* March 19. Available at https://www.psychologytoday.com/ca/contributors/avidan-milevsky-phd, accessed on January 7, 2023.

Robberson, T. (2020). I looked the man (Putin) in the eye and saw …the enemy. *The Dallas Morning News.*

Sacks, V. & Murphy, D. (2018). The prevalence of adverse childhood experiences, nationally, by state, and by race or ethnicity. *Child Trends,* February 12. Available at https://www.childtrends.org/publications/prevalence-adverse-childhood-experiences-nationally-state-race-ethnicity, accessed on January 10, 2023.

Stevens, J.E. (2022). How Vladimir Putin's childhood is affecting us all. *Aces Too High News (Aces = Adverse Childhood Experiences),* March 2. Available at https://acestoohigh.com/2022/03/02/how-vladimir-putins-childhood-is-affecting-us-all/, accessed on January 6, 2023.

Tiramillas.com (adapted by Sam). (2022). Who is Vera Putina, the 96-year-old who claims to be Vladimir Putin's biological mother? *Marca,* March 30. Available at https://www.marca.com/en/lifestyle/world-news/2022/03/30/6244442046163f25948b45a2.html, accessed on January 17, 2022.

U.S. Center for Disease Control and Prevention. (2023). Adverse childhood experiences (ACEs). Available at https://www.cdc.gov/violenceprevention/aces/index.html, accessed on January 29, 2023.

Wikipedia. (2022). Vera Putina. Available at https://en.wikipedia.org/wiki/Vera_Putina, accessed on January 17, 2022.

Willock, B. (in preparation). *The Colonel and the Cannibal.*

Winnicott, D.W. (1963). Communicating and not communicating leading to a study of certain opposites. In D.W. Winnicott (Ed.), *The Maturational Process and the Facilitating Environment.* London: Hogarth, pp. 179–192.

Winnicott, D.W. (1965). *Maturational Processes and the Facilitating Environment.* New York: International Universities Press.

Zolotov, A. (2002). Putin offers reporter a circumcision. *The Moscow Times,* November 13. Available at https://www.themoscowtimes.com/2002/11/13/putin-offers-reporter-a-circumcision-a242217, accessed January 7, 2023.

Chapter 4

The "Empire of Lies"

Russia's War in Ukraine

Coline Covington

Invasion

My discussion of blame and collective guilt would not be complete without an attempt to understand the political dynamics and rationale of Russia's invasion of Ukraine on 24 February 2022. While some Russia experts had anticipated this would happen, it nevertheless came as a blow to Western nations and presented an imminent threat to Eastern European countries that had been within the Soviet bloc and those countries, such as Poland, bordering Russia. The invasion also elicited a certain amount of dismay within NATO countries and the US that Russia's invasion of Crimea in 2014 had virtually gone unchallenged. It had been a wake-up call that had been largely dismissed at the cost of Ukraine's safety.

In his speech marking the invasion of Ukraine, Putin laid out a clear narrative outlining the events that had in his view, cumulatively, given Russia no choice but to defend itself. Putin's list of Western threats and territorial aggression in Eastern Europe not only provided the justification for Russia's response but described a history of Russian humiliation, betrayal and victimhood – wounds that remain painful in Russian memory. In particular, Putin cites Russia's grievances against deceitful Western governments. Referring to the collapse of the Soviet Union and increasing efforts by the West to encircle and destroy Russia, Putin stated:

> … This array includes promises not to expand NATO eastward even by an inch. To reiterate: They have deceived us, or, to put it simply, they have played us.

Within this narrative, Putin accused the West and the US of supporting separatist groups, such as in Chechnya, attempting to divide and weaken Russia.

> This is how it was in the 1990s and the early 2000s, when the so-called collective West was actively supporting separatism and gangs of mercenaries in southern Russia. What victims, what losses we had to sustain and what trials we had to go through at that time before we broke the back of international terrorism in the Caucasus! We remember this and will never forget.

DOI: 10.4324/9781003376811-4

In building his case for the invasion of Ukraine, Putin mounted a series of "false flags" that described a projected cultural and political enemy that must be vanquished in order to preserve Russian territory and "to defend people who have been victims" under Kyiv's regime.[1] Putin went further to claim that it was the neo-Nazis in Ukraine's regime, supported by NATO's leading countries, that were committing genocide on the Russian population. He explained:

> This brings me to the situation in Donbass. We can see that the forces that staged the coup in Ukraine in 2014 have seized power, are keeping it with the help of ornamental election procedures and have abandoned the path of a peaceful conflict settlement. We had to stop that atrocity, that genocide of the millions of people who live there and who pinned their hopes on Russia, on all of us.

Putin also described the threat that NATO countries "who will never forgive the people of Crimea and Sevastopol for freely making a choice to reunite with Russia," would not stop with Ukraine but would go on to attack Crimea. He predicted the slaughter of "innocent people just as members of the punitive units of Ukrainian nationalists and Hitler's accomplices did during the Great Patriotic War. They have also openly laid claim to several other Russian regions." Putin's words were a forewarning of his own ambitions to recover what were once considered Russian regions.

The most powerful message in Putin's speech is the claim that Russia is facing an existential threat and has no choice but to fight for its identity and ultimate survival.

> For our country, it is a matter of life and death, a matter of our historical future as a nation…It is not only a very real threat to our interests but to the very existence of our state and to its sovereignty. It is the red line which we have spoken about on numerous occasions. They have crossed it.

Putin finally emphasized:

> If we look at the sequence of events and the incoming reports, the showdown between Russia and these forces cannot be avoided. It is only a matter of time. They are getting ready and waiting for the right moment. Moreover, they went as far as to aspire to acquire nuclear weapons. They did not leave us any other option for defending Russia and our people, other than the one we are forced to use today. In these circumstances, we have to take bold and immediate action.

As we were soon to discover, Putin's words were prophetic – but prophetic in a paranoid reality, projecting an exaggerated mirror image on to Ukraine and the West of Putin's own intentions and worldview. It has been striking that every announcement Putin has made referring to his predictions of Western aggression have

The "Empire of Lies": Russia's War in Ukraine   71

in fact signalled his next moves, as if he is transmitting these in advance not only as a justification for his actions but as a provocation which, if acted upon, would validate Russia's position as the victim.

Blame and Truth

Invasion by a foreign country is profoundly traumatic for any nation and leaves its own trace of vulnerability and fear. The invasions of Russia by the Mongols in the thirteenth century, by Napoleon in 1812, and Hitler in 1941 have left deep scars on the Russian psyche – scars that have made Russia particularly anxious about its survival as a state. Putin's repetitive presentation of Russia as a "besieged fortress" underscores the shame and humiliation of the Russian people. By exacerbating the history of Russian humiliation, Putin fosters Russian identification with the victim and the consequent rationale for retaliation.

When a nation's sovereignty and identity are under threat, it seeks to protect and strengthen itself by keeping alive in its collective memory the "chosen traumas" that mark so much of its history and, inevitably, its identity. Within these "chosen traumas," the archetype of the heroic martyr who sacrifices his life for his Mother country is idealized and used to inspire a vision of recovery and a future as great as the past. Alongside the "chosen traumas" are the "chosen glories" that signify the potency and successes of the past and the imperial glory that can be regained and turned to as a curative revenge for humiliation. "Chosen traumas" are also sites of blame and warnings to be alert to further attacks from foreigners who are not to be trusted.

Blame is a recurring theme in Russian history that speaks to many Russians today. While typically blame is cast or ascribed to the enemy without, there is also a certain tradition of blamelessness within the country that reflects a history of apathy and impotence to effect change. The question, "who's to blame?," first came into common parlance with the publication of Alexander Herzen's novel *Who's to Blame*, in 1847. The novel was a social and psychological commentary on contemporary life in Russia – amongst the first literary works of its kind.[2] It depicts three good characters who are destroyed by an array of social causes that were not of their own making. The characters are impotent to influence the events in their lives, as individuals they are merely "a chip of wood floating on a river" (quoted in Grenier, 1995). The overwhelming complexity of the social problems faced by the Russian characters in the novel defeats their ability to act with any self-agency. Herzen's argument suggests that those who have no ability to effect social change, much less evaluate what needs to be done, cannot be held responsible for actions of the state. As the individual, and the group, lack any realizable social responsibility, they are in effect blameless vis-à-vis moral judgment.

While Herzen's citizens lacked the self-agency to act in any meaningful way politically, it is questionable how much self-agency Russians feel they have today. State control of the media is a powerful tool to quell dissent and dissent can have serious consequences in any case. Propaganda, however, does not necessarily induce trust in leadership. Recent research indicates that Putin's manipulation of information and the press is more likely to produce political apathy than actual approval. Distrust of propaganda has a deleterious effect that undermines people's capacity for moral judgment and in turn creates a sense of political impotence.

The political scientist, Maxim Alyukov, maintains that autocratic regimes no longer rely chiefly on physical violent repression to create obedience amongst their populations but achieve this through the ways in which media is harnessed to present conflicting narratives that lead to generalized distrust of information.[3] Alyukov comments, "Instead of making citizens trust regime narratives, propaganda often capitalizes on media distrust. Media trust in autocracies is usually low, because citizens are aware that media are manipulated" (Alyukov, 2022). Rather than making citizens question what information they can trust, the effect of propaganda, especially when conflicting narratives are available, is to create distrust of all media. As Alyukov writes:

> This belief in the propagandistic nature of the Russian state media spills over into questioning the very possibility of objective reporting. Although Russian state media attempt to impose a specific interpretation of the Russia–Ukraine conflict, one of the central messages of these narratives is not 'trust our interpretation of the conflict', but instead 'you cannot trust any interpretation'. This strategy further exacerbates widespread distrust towards the media, which in turn amplifies support for the war. The following passage from an interview with a professed supporter illustrates how distrust towards the media makes the respondent support, rather than oppose, the war: "I cannot say that I support [the war] because I am against the war. But I cannot say that I am against it either because I think that I do not have enough information. The news is just brainwashing people [...] But what I can say for sure is that I will not openly say 'I am against' until [the war] is over. When it is over, we will discuss it. But now I am a citizen of my country. Let my country finish what it is doing – even without my approval." When no information can be trusted, the respondent defaults to national identity.
>
> (Alyukov, 2022)

Hannah Arendt pointed out that when unquestioning adherence to the party line is expected, regardless of what is true or not, then nothing is trustworthy, and no one can make up their minds. It deprives the group of being able to think and judge – and ultimately to act (Arendt, 1967). However, as the Serbian scholar Dzihic argues, bewildering stories and lies "throws dust in the eyes of the public" and can be even more effective in reinforcing the group's subservience to an autocratic leader[4] (quoted in NYR Daily, The Age of Total Lies, V. Pesic and C. Simic, 6/2/17).

The "Empire of Lies": Russia's War in Ukraine   73

These findings throw into question the extent to which the Russian population actively supports Putin's war of aggression in Ukraine and what opinion polls are actually reflecting.[5] While younger generations, increasingly urbanized and who have had greater exposure to the West, are more likely to challenge Putin's actions, it is hard to differentiate between others who endorse the regime's narrative and those who remain silent out of distrust. It also raises a more fundamental question about collective responsibility.

The Chosen Myth

The dissolution of the Soviet Union marked the end of communism and socialist ideology. By the time Putin came to power as Prime Minister on 9 August 1999, Russian political ideology was virtually non-existent. The following two decades saw Russia's economy thrive. With increased exposure to the West came increased awareness of civil rights and political freedoms heretofore unavailable. What was notable during this time was the absence of a guiding political ideology or vision of Russia.[6]

The Belorussian journalist, Svetlana Alexievich, in her book *Second-Hand Time* (2013), documents a bitter nostalgia across generations and classes for the political beliefs that had inspired them to live with hardship and deprivation in the past. She writes about the communist vision to remake the

> old breed of man....Seventy-plus years in the Marxist-Leninist laboratory gave rise to a new man: *Homo sovieticus*....People who come out of socialism are both like and unlike the rest of humanity – we have our own lexicon, our own conceptions of good and evil, our heroes and martyrs. We have a special relationship with death.
>
> (2013, p. 23)

When it was all over, as one woman complained,

> All of our suffering was in vain....It's terrible to admit it and even worse to live with it. All of our gruelling labour! We built so much. Everything with our own hands. The times we lived through were so hard!....After Stalin died, people started smiling again; before that, they lived carefully. Without smiles.
>
> (Ibid., p. 141)

And yet, having lived through these hard times, this woman also decried a new world empty of meaning. She said, "Nobody believes in anything any more. Not in the *domovoi*,[7] and not in communism. People live without any kind of faith!" (Ibid., p. 139).

Snyder, a historian, describes the collapse at the end of the Soviet Union of what he terms the "politics of inevitability" that holds the promise of a better future. All the suffering of those years in the name of communism and for what? The "politics of inevitability" was superseded by what Synder refers to as the "politics of eternity." Snyder writes:

> Eternity places one nation at the center of a cyclical story of victimhood. Time is no longer a line into the future, but a circle that endlessly returns the same threats from the past. Within inevitability, no one is responsible because we all know that the details will sort themselves out for the better; within eternity, no one is responsible because we all know that the enemy is coming no matter what we do. Eternity politicians spread the conviction that government cannot aid society as a whole but can only guard against threats. Progress gives way to doom.
>
> (Snyder, 2018, p. 8)

With the demise of socialist ideology and a utopian view of the future, we can see how Putin has created a "historic future" that is based on the return of the past and centres around the safeguarding of Russia's identity.

Certainly, Putin is no ideologue.[8] Strongly influenced by the Russian fascist philosopher, Ivan Ilyin, and Russian ethnologist, Lev Gumilev, Putin has resuscitated the identity of imperial Russia – of a Russia that harks back to the Mongols and spans the breadth of Eurasia. As Putin announced, "The Eurasian union is a project meant to preserve the identities of nations and the historic Eurasian community in the new century, in a new world." It could be the Soviet Union reincarnate, the significant difference being that alliance rests on the core identification of being Eurasian rather than Soviet. It is not a political union; it is a quasi-spiritual ethnic union binding Russia together. From what was an ideological vacuum, Putin has injected a vision of a mythic past to bolster Russia's ailing identity. This has also enabled Putin to blame his predecessors, Lenin and Stalin, for creating the concept of the Soviet Union that granted a degree of local autonomy that ultimately, according to Putin, caused the schisms within the state that resulted in its breakup.

Putin's vision of a Eurasian community encompasses Ilyin's conception of Russia as "an organism of nature and the soul," a virginal nation, "without original sin" (Snyder, 2018, p. 23). As such, the sovereignty of Ukraine and other territories tied to Russia historically becomes as inconceivable as separating a limb from a body and expecting it to continue to exist. Ilyin denied Ukraine's separate existence, assuming that it would be included in a post-Soviet Russia – acknowledging Ukraine as an independent entity was equivalent, in Ilyin's view, to being a "mortal enemy" of Russia (Ibid.). Prior to Russia's invasion of Ukraine, Putin echoed Ilyin's position, explaining that Ukraine was not a "real" county but was in fact part of Russia, sharing Russia's "own history, culture and spiritual space" (Putin's speech, 24 February 2022). Seen from this perspective, Russia's invasion of Crimea and Ukraine

The "Empire of Lies": Russia's War in Ukraine   75

is Putin's attempt to resurrect the empire that Peter the Great had established and to restore Russian purity. Putin's identification with Peter the Great should not be merely attributed to Putin's narcissism; it is a carefully constructed historical analysis that draws on the "chosen glories" of Russia's past to recreate and consolidate a particular "chosen myth." In the absence of ideology, Putin has turned to this "chosen myth" as a means of shaping Russian identity in the present.

Gumilev's influence on Putin and the creation of what I am calling the "chosen myth" has been apparent in Putin's emphasis on nationalistic values of sacrifice and loyalty in order to achieve the restoration of the Russian body. By May 2012, following his re-election as President, Putin had essentially transformed the Russian state according to Ilyin's proposals to create a constitutional autocracy.[9] In his annual speech, Putin warned against foreign interference in Russian politics, emphasizing that "Direct or indirect meddling in our internal political processes is unacceptable" (Reuters, "Putin, in Annual Address, Denounces Foreign Meddling," 12 December 2012). At the same time, Putin stressed the need to preserve "national and spiritual identity." But the real giveaway was when Putin referred to Gumilev's idea of "passionarnost."

"I would like all of us to understand clearly that the coming years will be decisive," said Putin, hinting, as he often does, at some massive future calamity.

> Who will take the lead and who will remain on the periphery and inevitably lose their independence will depend not only on the economic potential but primarily on the will of each nation, on its inner energy, which Lev Gumilev termed passionarnost: the ability to move forward and to embrace change.
>
> (Clover, 2016)

Fifteen months later, in March 2014, Russia invaded Crimea and the drive to incorporate breakaway states back into Russia began, leading to the war in eastern Ukraine. Putin's reference to "passionarnost" is important as it underpins the rationale for these acts of aggression within a spiritual, philosophical framework. The term itself refers to the human instinct manifest in groups to grow and expand, the internal energy of the ethnos, the driving force of cultural, political and geopolitical creation. This meaning conveys the belief that such a drive, because it is instinctual, is therefore natural and not a matter of choice or policy – it is the Russian spirit and indeed the will of the masses. As an instinctual drive, it also necessarily entails suffering, a condition that the Russian people are only too familiar with across centuries of hardship and differing political ideologies. As we see in Alexievich's accounts of nostalgia for Soviet Russia, suffering for a higher cause provides meaning to life for many people and is at the heart of the tradition of heroic sacrifice for the Motherland. While many Russians in the younger generations increasingly question this tradition and Putin's autocracy, the "chosen myth" Putin is expounding resonates with much of the Russian collective experience and psyche.

Through Putin's narcissistic historical lens, Russia is the perpetual victim that has had to continually struggle to protect herself from foreign enemies, to remain pure, and to be true to passionarnost, i.e., to the will of the ethnos. Snyder describes the shift in Russia from a propaganda of "inevitability," promoting the melioristic belief that everything will get better, to that of "eternity," of a nation besieged that must fight for its very existence. Government can no longer aid society or help it to progress; it can only protect society from threats of attack. With the notion of eternity, the idea of history collapses and the collective mentality remains fixed in a timeless paranoid-schizoid position; evil is always external and unceasing, the group always its innocent victim. As Snyder comments, "Progress gives way to doom" (Snyder, 2018, p. 8). The leader then assumes the role of saviour – the one who will rescue the nation through his actions and at the same time absolve the group of responsibility or judgment as this is not needed when the group is by definition innocent.

Collective Guilt?

The war in Ukraine highlights the complexities of applying concepts such as collective responsibility and collective guilt to a nation in which there is not only a certain amount of dissent but the information available through state-censored media is so manifestly distorted. Under an autocratic regime that allows for minimal dissent and in which decision making regarding foreign policy is largely, if not exclusively, in the hands of Putin and his immediate coterie, it is hard to confer responsibility for actions taken abroad on to the Russian population. Even more difficult when the population lacks trust in the information that is available and, lacking trust, they lack the means to judge.[10] We return to Hannah Arendt's point that without the ability to judge, we have no moral compass and are at the mercy of the leader who determines the truth. Without judgement and without responsibility, there can be no guilt – all remain innocent, free of moral wrongdoing and harm. As Graham Greene wryly comments in his novel, *The Quiet American*, "...you can't blame the innocent, they are always guiltless. All you can do is either control them or eliminate them. Innocence is a kind of insanity" (Greene, 1955, p. 216).

Putin's adherence to Gumilev's idea of passionarnost emphasizes the purity and innocence of the Russian people who have been victimized from time immemorial. In the case of Crimea and Ukraine, Russian acts of aggression are projected onto the "other," using false flag accusations in the name of self-defence. This schizoid or binary position also infects opponents of Putin's actions who condemn all Russians as morally culpable because of their country of origin. The parallel with Nazi Germany is all too evident. Racism rears its head on both sides in a mirror reflection and disables thinking and judgement. While nations and their leaders do have responsibility for their actions towards other nations and can be held accountable for these, ascribing guilt on to the population as a whole is a moralistic tool that is often just as discriminatory in its nature as the crime itself.

The "Empire of Lies": Russia's War in Ukraine   77

When innocence needs to be upheld so strongly, it can quickly, as Greene observes, tip over into madness and paranoia. While the US and the NATO alliance have taken great care not to escalate the war in Ukraine, particularly in the face of Putin's threats of nuclear attack, it is apparent that Putin is provoking the West to retaliate in order to further justify its position of being the besieged country. This is the classic position of the bully who gains power by accusing his opponent of being the bully. The real threat is Putin's insistence on his innocence, an innocence that must be defended at all costs.

Three days after the invasion of Ukraine and the announcement of sanctions on Russian banks, Dmitry Kiselyov, the host of Russia 1 flagship television news programme, announced against a background of film images of Russian strategic missile submarines going out to sea, "Our submarines are capable of launching over 500 nuclear warheads, which guarantees the destruction of the U.S. and all NATO countries…The principle is: Why do we need a world, if Russia is not in it?"

Kiselyov, often called "Putin's mouthpiece," was clearly conveying the message in his broadcast that there is no limit to Putin's resolve to protect Russia, even if it means that Russia goes down with the rest of the world (Homer-Dixon, 2022). Although many view Putin's threats as bluster and attempt to reassure themselves that no rational leader would actually behave in such a self-destructive way, these are dangerous assumptions that do not take account of the cultural tradition which Putin represents and a belief system that inspires suffering and sacrifice for the sake of the Motherland, extending back to the Mongols and across the breadth of Eurasia. Without this cultural knowledge, Putin's vision and his threats do seem irrational and can erroneously be put down to the rantings of a mythomane. But, as the suicidal end of Hitler's Reich has shown us, this view fails to recognize the insanity of collective innocence and the danger it poses to us all.

Notes

1 Putin's narrative of Ukrainian aggression directly echoes Hitler's justification for invading Poland in September 1939. Nazi propagandists accused Poland of persecuting ethnic Germans living in Poland. The parallel with Putin's claim that Ukraine is persecuting its Russian citizens is evident.
2 Gogol's play *The Government Inspector* was originally published in 1836 with a revised edition published in 1842 when his short story *The Overcoat* came out. Dostoevsky's novel *Poor Folk* was published in 1846.
3 Alyukov's argument distinctly focuses on the role of distrust in subjugating citizens. For a detailed description of the move from violent repression to information manipulation as a more effective form of civil control, see Guriev, S. & Treisman, D. (2022). *Spin Dictators: The Changing Face of Tyranny in the 21st Century.* Princeton, NJ: Princeton University Press.
4 The effect of media distrust in silencing civil dissent is not only a phenomenon of authoritarian regimes but is also clearly evident in democratic societies, such as the United States, beleaguered with "fake" news.
5 Following the invasion of Ukraine, the Levada Center opinion poll reported an increase in Putin's approval ratings to 71%, nearly reaching his highest rating of 79% in May 2018.

6　See Chapter 8 in Covington, C. (2021). *For Goodness Sake: Bravery, Patriotism and Identity*. Phoenix Publishing House.
7　House goblin of Russian folklore.
8　A Kremlin consultant claims Putin "hates the word ideology" (quoted in Guriev, S. & Treisman, D. (2022). *Spin Dictators: The Changing Face of Tyranny in the 21st Century*. Princeton, NJ: Princeton University Press. P. 75.)
9　For Ilyin, the leader and redeemer of the people was a "democratic dictator." Freedom of the individual accordingly meant submission to the collective and subjugation to its leader (see Snyder, p. 47).
10　This is not to say that large groups are not collectively responsible for their actions, but that responsibility is not a categorical concept but contingent on a number of social factors. It is also not to say that democratic societies are more responsible collectively than autocratic societies.

References

Alexievich, S. (2013). *Second-Hand Time*. London: Fitzcarraldo Editions.
Alyukov, M. (2022). "Propaganda, authoritarianism and Russia's invasion of Ukraine." *Nature Human Behaviour*, 6, 763–765.
Arendt, H. (25 February 1967). "Truth and Politics." *New Yorker*.
Clover, C. (11 March 2016). "Lev Gumilev: passion, Putin and power." *Financial Times*.
Greene, G. (1955). *The Quiet American*. London: Vintage Classics.
Grenier, S. (Spring 1995). "Herzen's Who is to Blame? The Rhetoric of the New Morality." *The Slavic and East European Journal*, 39(**1**).
Guriev, S. & Treisman, D. (2022). *Spin Dictators: The Changing Face of Tyranny in the 21st Century*. Princeton, NJ: Princeton University Press. P. 44
Homer-Dixon, T. (10 March 2022). "Two things the West must do to lower the probability that Putin will pull the nuclear trigger." *Cascade Institute*.
Snyder, T. (2018). *The Road to Unfreedom: Russia, Europe, America*. London: The Bodley Head.

Chapter 5

The Leader-Follower Relationship

Richard Wood

Numerous clinicians have explored nature of the leader-follower relationship in the context of pathological leadership. As I review this literature, the reader will see that there is a great deal of shared commonality in the formulations that various authors have developed.

In 1964, Eric Fromm wrote that pathological narcissism – what he referred to as malignant narcissism – could express itself in large groups of people just as it could in individuals. He called such group narcissism "social narcissism," saying that "it plays as a source of violence and war" (p. 75). He emphasized that:

> The survival of the group depends to some extent on the fact that its members consider its importance as great or greater than that of their own lives, and furthermore that they believed in the righteousness, or the superiority, of their group as compared with others.
>
> (p. 75)

Being part of such a group allowed one to experience oneself as superior or special to a degree that such an identification might represent "the only – often very effective – source of satisfaction" (p. 75) for those members of a given society who could be seen to be culturally or economically disadvantaged. In such a group, reason and scientific attitude were likely to be experienced as imperiling the group's narcissistic belief system. Compromised rationality and objectivity were the "most obvious and frequent symptoms" (p. 81) of pathological group narcissism.

As previously mentioned in Chapter 1, Fromm considered that "incestuous symbiosis" (p. 91) was one of a triad of forces, which also included pathological narcissism and a necrophilous orientation (one opposed to life-giving/enhancing activity), that informed malignant narcissism. He asserted that:

> This incestuous striving, in the pre-genital sense, is one of the most fundamental passions in men and women, comprising the human being's desire for protection, the satisfaction of his narcissism; his craving to be freed from the risks of

DOI: 10.4324/9781003376811-5

responsibility, of freedom, of awareness; his longing for unconditional love, which is offered without any expectation of his loving response.

(p. 93)

Such a striving also represented a powerful motive force in mature men and women, particularly when they were subjected to exquisite vulnerabilities that life could generate within them. As a result, humankind was susceptible to symbiotic yearning that affiliation with clan, nation, race, religion, or God could offer. As I noted in my book, Fromm believed that surrendering to a powerful other and to a group was a "fraught process, one imbued with the promise of ecstasy and with the threat of annihilation to the self" (p. 13). Being part of such a group meant that one could be possessed of power, authority, and the means to protect oneself and one's loved ones; it also carried with it the potentiality of a dying of the self as one surrendered parts of the self to the larger group identity. Fromm again underscored that, like receptivity to a pathologically narcissistic leader, gratifying the desire for symbiotic union necessarily required one to back away from independence of thought and judgement so that one could embrace interpretations of reality that the larger group subscribed to. In compensation, one was protected from the aloneness that discernment and critical thinking could create.

Kernberg's (1989) understanding of large group dynamics mediated by malignant narcissistic leadership echoed many of the themes which Fromm identified:

Under conditions of social upheaval, turmoil or stress and in the presence of a powerful paranoid leadership, the group (can shift) into the opposite extreme of endorsing a primitive, powerful, sadistic leader who will assure the group that, by identifying collectively with the threatening primitive aggression he incorporates, they will be safe from persecution by becoming persecutors themselves.

(p. 202)

What I find interesting about these comments is Kernberg's acknowledgement that those people who join with the malignant narcissistic leader incorporate much of his aggression, turning it towards others who, by implication, are relatively more vulnerable to predation.

In two later papers on sanctioned social violence (2003a, 2003b), Kernberg highlighted the inherent narcissistic and paranoid regressive pull of such a group that could instigate both tyranny and violence. He noted that in such a group the regressive pull drew group members back towards latency age functioning which Kernberg understood was

characterized by concrete distinctions between good and bad, diminished tolerance for ambivalence and ambiguity, a reduction of relationships to idealized and persecutory figures, assumption of a primitive morality…, profound repression of the linkage between eroticism and tenderness in sexuality, analization of sexuality linking sex with excretory functions, an inability to tolerate emotional depth, and a desire to consolidate autonomy and, by implication identity, by embracing the mores and values that group membership offers.

(p. 689)

Kernberg considered that people susceptible to pathological leadership might be drawn to the narcissistic leader in a chaotic or confused social context; a paranoid leader when the group faced significant threat; and a malignantly narcissistic leader who demonstrated a "pathological condensation of narcissistic and paranoid features..." when social threat was maximal (p. 690). He further explained that paranoid ideology that "explains to a mass its origin and sense, its purpose and future, may contribute to the severe paranoid regression of an entire community or entire nation" (p. 690). Although he did not explicitly say so, at least in part the implications of his remarks suggested that the more severe and subjectively injurious the threats that a given culture had endured, the more likely it was to choose a leader to represent its interests whose sense of personal threat and mistrust mirrored that of the group. Kernberg explained that:

The leader characterized by malignant narcissism experiences and expresses an inordinate grandiosity, needs to be loved, admired, feared, and submitted to at the same time, cannot accept submission from others except when it is accompanied by intense idealizing loyalty and abandonment of all independent judgement, and experiences any manifestation contrary to his wishes as a sadistic, wilful, grave attack against himself.

(p. 693, part 1)

Kernberg believed that the community which the malignant narcissist led could be seen to consist of "totally subservient, idealizing subjects, with totally corrupted ruthless antisocial characters whose pretense of loving and submitting to the leader permits their parasitic enjoyment of his power" (p. 695) He iterated defeat in war, persecution of a religious minority, brutal suppression by an alternative racial group, historical trauma associated with transgenerational effects, any breakdown or disorganization of a "traditional, powerfully structured and socially stable system of government ..." (p. 695) as potential causative factors that could be seen to create receptivity to malignant narcissistic leadership.

Kohut (1976) proposed the concept of a "group self" (p. 837) whose dynamics would be subject to many of the same forces that governed individual dynamics. Like Kernberg and Fromm, he maintained that group pressure diminishes individuality and "leads to a primitivization of the mental processes" (p. 839) that could potentiate "cathartic expression of archaic... impulses, emotions, and ideation..." (p. 839). He believed that as one extended an understanding of individual dynamics to the group, one could "observe the group self as it is formed, as it is held together, as it oscillates between fragmentation and reintegration, as it shows regressive behaviour when it moves towards fragmentation…" (p. 838). He thought such an understanding might permit a "contribution to the explanation of historical events, of the course… of history" (p. 836). In elaborating his concerns about pathological forms of narcissistic leadership in his paper "On Leadership (1969–70)," he cautioned that:

> Narcissistic leader figures of this type experience the social surroundings as part of themselves. The mere fact that other groups, nationalities, or races are different from themselves, do not react as they expect them to react is a deep personal affront, the frightening, inimitable disturbance of their solipsistic universe. The situation can only be remedied by wiping out those who dare to be different.
>
> (p. 107)

As had Kernberg, he warned that the pathologically narcissistic leader imbued with paranoia was potentially particularly destructive because "(group members) are principally united by their sharing of an archaic narcissistic conception of the world that must destroy those who are different and by the identity of the grandiose fantasies embodied in their leader" (p. 107). Like both Kernberg and Fromm, he concluded that individuals who had suffered painful narcissistic injuries might "seek to melt into the body of a powerful nation (as symbolized by a grandiose leader) to cure their shame and provide them with the feeling of enormous strength, to which they react with relief and triumph" (p. 110). He also added that "the most malignant human propensities are mobilized in support of nationalistic narcissistic rage" (p. 117).

Mika (2017) identified societal conditions likely to generate followers prepared to embrace malignant narcissistic leadership. Such conditions included oppressive economic realities, social inequality, a breakdown of social norms, and a "growing disregard for the humanity of a large part of the population and for higher values" (pp. 300–301). In her view, effected societies could be expected to demonstrate "an inevitable split in their grandiose and their devalued parts and denial of the shadow, which is projected outward on others" (p. 301). Ian Hughes (2019) echoed Mika's and others' beliefs that dangerous personalities were likely to captivate leadership when the governed had absorbed unendurable narcissistic wounds, often in the form of wealth inequality, profound humiliation, or the social degradation of being dispossessed of dignity, security, and respect. Dangerous personalities at these times of vulnerability were felt to be particularly attractive because they conveyed authority, certainty, and an ability to act decisively in an unfettered way to solve problems.

In his chapter in "The Dangerous Case of Donald Trump," Jerrold Post (2019) felt that the "sense of grandiose omnipotence of the leader is especially appealing to his or her needy followers" and that "a hallmark of destructive charismatic leaders is absolutist, polarizing rhetoric, drawing their followers together against the outside enemy" (p. 385). He argued – only somewhat in contrast to other clinicians – that "in times of crisis, individuals regress to a state of delegated omnipotence and demand a leader (who will rescue them, take care of them)" (p. 388).

The Leader-Follower Relationship 83

He asserted that "the leader is the creation of his followers" and that "individuals susceptible to (the hypnotic attraction of) charismatic leadership have themselves fragmented or weak ego structures" (p. 388). Later in his chapter he suggested that early developmental trauma could produce individuals who felt incomplete unto themselves who could "only feel whole when in a relationship, attached, or merged with this idealized other" (p. 393). He described what he referred to as "two vicissitudes of wounded self" (p. 388). The "mirror hungry personality" (p. 388) was reflective of a leader who feeds on the adorations of his followers. Its reciprocal, the "ideal hungry personality" referred to followers who "can experience themselves as worthwhile only so long as they can relate to individuals whom they can admire for their prestige, power, beauty, intelligence, or moral stature" (p. 390). The inner doubts and misgivings of the ideal hungry personality are offset by the "wall of dogmatic certainty" that the mirror hungry personality projects. As had others, Post, referencing Phyllis Greenacre, confirmed that "in order to be effectively charismatic it is a great asset to possess paranoid conviction," adding that "although there is no necessary relationship between charisma and paranoia, when the two are linked some of the most fearful excesses of human violence in history have occurred" (p. 392). He attributed these ideas to Robert Robbins' 1984 paper "Paranoia and Charisma." Post also identified group membership as a means to assuage aloneness and to create identity.

In his landmark work *The Authoritarian Personality*, Theodor Adorno et al. (1950) argued that specific forms of parenting, particularly a harsh and punitive parental presence, was likely to create a personality that sought approval from authority figures through obeisance and accommodation. Such personalities were expected to demonstrate blind accommodation to conventional morality, a willingness to unquestioningly accept the dictates of authority, and an inclination to attack others who resisted authority.

Hannah Arendt conceived of the concept banality of evil after listening to Adolf Eichmann give evidence at his own trial ("Eichmann in Jerusalem," 1963). She was struck by his readiness to allow himself to be defined by the values of the societal context in which he was immersed rather than permitting himself to remain vested in his own humanity, i.e., to think and to feel, as she would call it. Dabrowski et al. (1973) warned about the danger of education that promotes adherence to conventionality and Fromm (1941) invited us to consider how uncomfortable freedom of choice was for us and to what lengths we might go to sidestep it.

Ever since Stanley Milgram's famous Yale study (1963) demonstrating our readiness to accept and carry out the dictates of an authoritarian other even if in so doing we create harm and even lethality, the social sciences have been preoccupied by the ease with which authority can seduce us. We are still looking for answers that would help us better understand our terrible vulnerability to an authoritarian other.

At this juncture in this chapter, I would now like to review my own appreciation of the leader-follower relationship, which the reader will see is in some ways unique and in others draws heavily upon the work which has preceded my own.

The malignant narcissistic leader's realities are such that he can never feel safe, though he would deny a sense of vulnerability, experiencing it as distasteful and diminishing and, probably on a largely unconscious basis, as an intolerable affront to the grandiosity and omnipotence that binds his personality together. Accordingly, he projects obdurate 'strength' and certainty, using an outsized voice infected with irresistible conviction that conveys he, above all others, is possessed of the answers that a beleaguered, frightened, or humiliated populace is searching for. In the process, he may manufacture crises that inflame others' vulnerabilities – perhaps much as Putin did through the Chechen threat – crises that further draw those he would govern to stand by his side and begin to suborn themselves to his voice. He speaks directly to their fear and alienation, which creates an illusion of empathic attunement that belies his profound self-interest. As others have noted, his message is likely to beguile those who have suffered any of a broad range of calamities that could include war, economic privation, devastating natural calamities, real or manufactured indignities attributed to a governing elite, perceived threat represented by either internal or external forces portrayed as jeopardizing a state and its people or cultural disruption occasioned by potentially disparate sources (as examples, breakdown of government – particularly relevant to the Russian situation – or waves of immigration).

His appeal offers a frightened, diminished population the opportunity to transform its fear into rage and indignation to be directed against designated targets. Fear that permeates the governed, in other words, is readily and cynically exploited by the malignant narcissist. He invites them to engage in punitive acts of aggression towards those he identifies as enemies. In so doing he confirms his constituents' power and authority and his own. Their newfound sense of agency promises resolution of chaos, reaffirms identity, creates a strong sense of community for the formerly dispossessed, and re-establishes a sense of safety for people whose own vulnerability and depreciation was felt to have become unendurable. He is also appealing to those he would govern to bask in his sense of aggrandizement, participating in the omnipotence and grandiosity he assigns to himself and would share with them. For people in pain and/or for people receptive, by virtue of their cultural givens, to an autocratic voice, the bargain that he offers them might seem well nigh irresistible – particularly in a context in which he conveys that the alienation which defines them also defines him.

I think the siren call of autocracy is also compelling for other, broader reasons, some of which may be embedded in long-standing social realities that characterize a particular culture or people. I am referring to humanity's inherent discomfort with the chaotic, frequently frightening landscapes that typify our inner lives. We are beset by strong, contradictory feelings and images that challenge that which we hold most dear – our relationship with ourselves and our relationship with others. How do we accommodate ourselves to seemingly ungovernable impulses and feelings that threaten our own and others' existence? Often we reach accommodation by walling off that which we find unacceptable in ourselves. We rely on the rules and traditions that govern our cultures that help us accomplish this end – systems of laws, morals, and values that convey to us who we are supposed to be, how we are supposed to act, and what we are supposed to feel. Autocratic forms of government and autocratic institutions, like religions, have helped provide us with the boundaries that we need in order to feel safe with ourselves and with each other. We turn to them for guidance and clarity to help us manage the morass of potentially destructive feelings and urges that informs such a big part of the human experience. Someone else – the authoritative other or the authoritarian state – now bears the responsibility of deciding for us who we can become and what we can express. The state can tell us when we can express the dark parts of ourselves and when we must restrain them. We are freed from the necessity of having to assume responsibility for parts of the self that we would find too disconcerting to mediate for ourselves. I would argue that the more culturally sanctioned walls we have constructed inside ourselves, the more susceptible we are to submission to an authoritarian voice. Cultures that promote appreciation of individuality, openness to internal experience, and respect for diversity, in contrast, help protect their members from compliance to subjugation. I do not begin to know enough about the intricacies and the feel of Russian culture nor its history to consider where Russia might fall on the spectrum that I have described. I would only say I can see that contemporary Russian history has extended reliance on an authoritarian presence largely up to the point that Putin became president, possibly with the exception of Russia's brief foray into democracy.

There is another overarching reason which I would like to mention that I think makes its own substantial contribution to receptivity to the authoritarian other: that is, I would say, our compulsion to create meaning and place for ourselves by joining a community. So far as I can see, affiliation is one of humanity's strongest drives. Being part of a group may create various substantial costs for us that, for example, compromise individuality and dignity, but those costs, heavy as they can sometimes be, are subjectively offset by the opportunity to participate in something larger than ourselves. Membership in an autocratic group may offer us the means to resolve important existential questions. Not only are we part of something bigger than ourselves. That bigger than ourselves entity frequently assigns us a clearly defined hierarchical position that we are expected to fulfil. In so doing we are rewarded for the contribution that we make, and we get to consolidate a sense of meaning as part of a seemingly dynamic whole. In fulfilling our duties and in making the sacrifices required of us, we may even get to offset preoccupation with our own mortality.

In addition to the benefits of affiliation that I have just described, affiliation offers us an essential if not core source of sustenance for ourselves and, perhaps, the best means that many of us have to restore homeostasis and a sense of safety in the face of stress or fear arousal. As referenced in the literature review, for those people who struggle with the exquisite pain of an incomplete or emaciated self, group membership feels like a lifeline one is impelled to embrace – perhaps almost indiscriminately – as a means of relieving the pain that their personal impoverishment creates for them.

And, finally, receptivity to pathological leadership is also occasioned by our relative lack of knowledge about ourselves. While humankind has made great progress in knowing itself better, there remains a great deal for us to learn and to face about ourselves. Looking into the self, as I implied when I described the challenges of living, as we all do, with a chaotic, contradictory, seemingly reckless interior populated by disturbing images and impulses, is a daunting undertaking. Even in the context of a psychotherapy relationship in which the therapist makes assiduous efforts to create safety for the patient, there are many facets of the self that must remain unexplored, even when therapy has endured over prolonged periods of time. As Dr. Austin Ratner has suggested (2022), the stuff of which we are made is not straight and perfect but rather crooked and, one could add, oft times ill-formed. Our relative lack of self-awareness – which I would say is an inevitable part of the human condition – renders us all too accessible to those who would play upon our poorly understood personal vulnerabilities.

In accepting the Faustian bargain the autocrat offers us, we incur terrible and often unanticipated, escalating damage to ourselves and to the human community.

Those costs arise, in part, because the malignant narcissist's existence is such a precarious one. His identity is built around the grandiosity and omnipotence that he establishes for himself. It provides his personality with cohesion and, however improbably, a measure of stability. As such, he must protect the outsized, outlandish version of himself that he invests in personally and that he must constantly sell to the rest of the world. On the face of it, it looks like an impossible proposition. He's always got to be smarter, bigger, better, and possessed of more expertise than the people around him. Even if he is characterized by remarkable talent, he must inevitably find himself falling short at some points in his journey. When he does, no one must be allowed to see what has happened – including himself. Cracks in grandiosity and omnipotence, as previously discussed, may incite panic which quickly becomes rage. Underneath the overblown façade is the frightened, helpless child beset by intolerable threat I have suggested the malignant narcissist once was. Re-experiencing that part of himself would create intolerable jeopardy (what I referred to in my book as regression to an earlier ego state). Safety is achieved only through continuous assertion of strength and threat. Collaboration and constructive interdependence is largely or virtually entirely out of reach, particularly as his malignant narcissistic posture increasingly consolidates itself over the course of his lifetime. His investment in grandiosity and omnipotence and in an intransigent posture demarcating "strength" means that it is unsafe for him to empower other people's voices and personalities. In order to protect himself, he must repeatedly demonstrate that he can overpower the other – quite a daunting proposition to fulfil day by day.

His concern about protecting exclusivity of voice introduces other challenges into his relationship with the governed. In order to seduce them to his side, he

The Leader-Follower Relationship   87

must take pains to authenticate their voices so that they can experience a bigger and more powerful version of themselves, but in the process of doing so, he must ensure that their sense of aggrandizement derives entirely from his voice rather than from a voice which grows out of their own individuality. He must attempt, in other words, to both enhance the other and suppress them at one and the same time.

His conundrum is compounded by his inability to receive meaningful sustenance from others. His walls are designed to keep others out and to diminish them. Openness, love, warmth, playfulness, and generosity of spirit – all those qualities that make our relationships with others meaningful – escape him. He lacks the reassurance that he is loved and valued, forsaking it for the projection of indomitability that he needs for himself. His starvation produces endemic envy and acquisitiveness. He requires insatiable supplies of everything but decency and love to try to fill himself. The predatory, greedy, ruthless internal world that he experiences induces him to imagine that everyone else is as rapacious and envious as he is himself. Everyone becomes an enemy or at least a potential one. No relationship can feel enduringly safe. Openness and genuine relatedness connote intolerable vulnerability. Denied the music of rewarding human interchange, he is relegated to contriving a self. His implacable mistrust of others means that he must test others endlessly, subjecting them to humiliation and violation as his only means – beside shared transactional value – of confirming loyalty. His inner world becomes increasingly populated by the carnage he inflicts on the people around him. Moreover, he isn't in a position to be able to make much sense of what is happening within him because it is too frightening to confront the devastation that is accruing inside. Instead, he asks himself and others to focus upon his compensatory gifts, i.e., his status as an infallible visionary and all-powerful strongman. Back up the Batmobile and blow smoke – over and over and over again. Promoting the same rickety song and dance meant to cow and seduce others and hide the hole in his soul.

His injuriousness only escalates with the passage of time, creating more and more damaged people around him that he has violated. The more alone he becomes, the more strident his reactions are to those who challenge him.

The precariousness that I have ascribed to the malignant narcissist's mode of being infects his relationship with the people he is governing and colours their relationship with themselves and with each other. The war footing that he unrelentingly maintains imposes itself upon them. Just as he is perpetually hypervigilant and wary, so, too, are they as his sovereignty extends itself through measures meant to elaborate his repression of the governed, denying them voice and individuality. His endemic fear, which he could not willingly articulate for himself, becomes theirs. The more he consolidates his power, the more ruthless he becomes, and the more ruthless he becomes, the more fear the governed must absorb into the own lives. He diverts their attention from their fears of retaliation and violation by creating ever more enemies – real and faux – both inside and outside the state, extending and reiterating the tactics he relied upon to ingratiate himself with his followers. Inviting them to transform the sense of threat and violation that they experience into rage that they can enact towards designated others becomes an endless process that never enjoys meaningful resolution. In such a fashion they can deepen their identification with his omnipotence and feel a greater measure of safety as they, too, find others in the state hierarchy they can bully. In the process, they may enjoy a momentary sense of relief, but at a cost to their own humanity in the form of dissociation and increasingly shuttered empathy. In the long run, everyone appreciates – at least subliminally – that the state's roving hatreds may eventually target them. That is as the malignant narcissist wishes. Pervasive fear serves him well, reminding everyone, time and again, that prerogatives of voice and action belong to him, not to them. To separate oneself from his voice is to target oneself for annihilation. Fear is the foundation upon which his domination rests.

As everyone lives with increasingly suffocating fear and both the rage and helplessness that it inspires, their own interiors, much like the malignant narcissist's, become blighted and ugly, gradually displacing their capacity for love and decency. The malignant narcissist's envy of love that he is largely unable to give or receive incrementally deconstructs people's ability to care about and trust one another. That which he is denied he would deny others. Decency and compassion are unbearable for him and so, too, they must be for the people he governs. His envy compels him to blight their souls in much the same way that his has been. In the process, the malignant narcissist is working a piece of dark magic, replacing a version of the self that people once occupied with one that is characterized by growing ruthlessness, starvation, and destructiveness. In this fashion, the malignant narcissist moves the state ever closer to his own psychopathic realities. Those living within the state are increasingly drawn towards acts of cruelty, bullying, and rapacity as a means of filling themselves and confirming their aliveness and their potency. Like the malignant narcissist, their horizon becomes defined by a growing number of potential enemies.

The governed also pay other costs. In a fear-drenched environment, capacity for reason and nuanced thought informed by empathy faces significant compromise. Thought process shaped by fear becomes dominated by simplistic, binary choices primarily intended to serve the function of helping the perceiver distinguish between friend and foe, same and other. The language of fear is visceral, guttural, and evocative, and it is easily persuaded by inducements to escalate fear and hatred. As a consequence, the malignant narcissist enjoys greater empowerment in his efforts to shape public perception. With the passage of time, as with so many of the other effects that have been described, degradation of thought and reason becomes both a habit of being and a culturally sanctioned means of addressing challenges. Degradation of thought and reason – particularly in the absence of compassion – also means that what is identified as a "problem" often ignores recognition of pressing human needs that otherwise ought to demand attention. People's appreciation of their own and others' humanity is blunted by the fear-drenched thought they habitually live with.

The Leader-Follower Relationship   89

All of the costs just described are further escalated by the malignant narcissist's choice of close associates. Selecting either individuals who have already tainted themselves through their own extensive acts of corruption or who willingly enact the bigotries and hatreds he assigns them, perhaps because they find common cause in his prejudice, he now has recourse to a group of people who are compromised in much the same ways that he is. These are the people, then, that he can share a modicum of trust with: people whose own moral lapses render them vulnerable to him should they ever decide to challenge him. His deeply compromised associates, in other words, not only provide him with a ready supply of targets towards whom he can defer blame; their corrupt practices also afford him endless opportunities to use their corruption to bend them to his will. This cadre of deeply ethically impaired people, many of whom share his taste for ruthlessness and cruelty, selects more people like themselves at lower levels of government. Hatred, bigotry, bullying, and kleptocracy proliferate in ever wider circles, infusing the lives of the governed with more suffocating fear and with habits of cynicism and exploitation; eventually ugliness and rapacity become institutionalized and reflexive, common sense wisdom that everyone assumes to be true. In response, everyone's sense of humanity faces further diminishment. And opportunities for the malignant narcissist to enact his brutalist policies are enhanced, supported by an ever-growing number of collaborators all too willing to carry out any act of violence or devastation that might impress itself upon him in any given moment.

Fear eclipses morality, independence of thought, and the courage that people need to separate themselves from the destructive autocratic voice. Adherence to conventionality displaces people's capacity to think and to feel their own and others' pain. Pervasive threat blunts empathy and compassion, replacing it with lockstep adherence to the ethics of regime: blind accommodation to a ruthless cultural surround. Therein lies safety. Identify with the tyrant or face annihilation. Independence of thought and feeling is someone else's prerogative. With the passage of time, people inevitably lose track of the precious human gifts they have surrendered to the autocratic presence they have either chosen to embrace or have been compelled to.

If autocratic leadership and generation of enemies leads to a physical war – as has happened in Chechnya and in the Ukraine – acts of war inevitably produce horrific moral lapses that those fighting in a war enact. Those that must live with what they did often find themselves consigned to a world of secrecy in which the only other people they can talk to about what they have done are others who have also engaged in horrific trespass. The stage is set for society to devolve into self-protective fragments, each of which assiduously guards its own constellation of sins. Recovery of humanity for a nation thusly affected becomes more challenging, particularly if the war in question has occasioned censure and approbation as a so-called "bad" war.

The costs that have just been identified do not include the intergenerational effort of rebuilding democratic institutions, of deconstructing prejudice, of repairing poorly understood society-wide psychological wounds, of addressing economic damage, of grieving and accommodating devastating losses to one's culture, of mitigating possibly irreversible damage to the environment, and of reconfiguring a fractured international community, all of which autocracy occasions. And it's important to keep in mind that the devastation which autocracy generates sets the stage for future chaos, deprivation, and disorder which future autocrats can exploit.

A Faustian bargain indeed. And one that humanity has all too willingly engaged generation after generation to address fear and narcissistic injury.

Without close acquaintance with the conditions that pervade Russian existence on a day-to-day basis, it is difficult to say where the Russian experience would now fall along the continuum that I have described in the leader-follower relationship. Masha Gessen's account of Russian realities up to the point at which she left the Russian Federation do suggest that tyranny is advancing itself in expected ways. Putin's considerable ability – through virtually absolute control of the media – to mask the costs of the severe oppression that now pervades the Russian landscape obscures our view. I would say that he would have it no other way. The various polls attesting to his popularity and the Russian people's endorsement of his policies are of little help; they are as tainted and as distorted as Russian election results. My appraisal is that he has successfully manipulated public opinion in the ways that he would like to; I would also guess that even though public consensus suggests he enjoys approval for many of his policies, possibly including his conduct of the war, the real costs that I have described in this chapter are nonetheless accumulating – costs that many Russians would have a great deal of difficulty articulating for themselves. One is also mindful that the person in the street who speaks up and raises objections imperils him or herself, denying us the opportunity to hear their voices.

References

Arendt, H. (1963). *Eichmann in Jerusalem: A report on the banality of evil*. New York: Penquin Books.

Dabrowski, K., Kawczak, A., & Sochanska, J. (1973). *The dynamics of concepts*. London, UK: Gryf Publications.

Fromm, E. (1941). *Escape from freedom*. New York: Farrar & Rinehart.

Fromm, E. (1964). *The heart of man*. New York: Harper & Row.

Hughes, I. (2019). Disordered minds: Democracy as a defense against dangerous personalities. In B. Lee (Ed.). *The dangerous case of Donald Trump* (2nd ed., pp. 446–457). New York: Thomas Dunne Books.

Kernberg, O. (1989). The temptations of conventionality. *The International Review of Psychoanalysis*, 18, 191–204.

Kernberg, O. (2003a). Sanctioned social violence: Part I. *The International Journal of Psychoanalysis*, 84(3), 693–698.

Kernberg, O. (2003b). Sanctioned social violence: Part II. *The International Journal of Psychoanalysis*, 84(4), 953–968.

Kohut, H. (1976). Creativeness, charisma, group psychology: Reflections on the self-analysis of Freud. In P.H. Ornstein (Ed.). *The search for the self* (vol. 2, pp. 743–843). New York: International Universities Press, Inc.

Mika, E. (2017). Who goes Trump? Tyranny as a triumph of narcissism. In B. Lee (Ed.). *The dangerous case of Donald Trump* (2nd ed., pp. 289–308). New York: Thomas Dunne Books.

Milgram, S. (1963). Behavioral study of obedience. *Journal of Abnormal and Social Psychology*, 67, 371–378.

Post, J.M. (2019). The charismatic leader follower relationship and Trump's base. In B. Lee (Ed.). *The dangerous case of Donald Trump* (2nd ed., pp. 385–396). New York: Thomas Dunne Books.

Ratner, A. (October 20, 2022). Dear Vladimir Putin: If You've Read Dostoevsky, You've Tragically Misunderstood Him. Retrieved April 14, 2023, from, https://lithub.com/dear-vladimir-putin-if-youve-read-dostoevsky-youve-tragically-misunderstood-him/

Chapter 6

Vladimir Putin and the Pathologies of Modernity

Ian Hughes

Two Tales of Modernity

Two tales of modernity co-exist in the global public imagination. The first tale tells of modernity as humanity's awakening from ignorance and superstition thanks to science and reason and escape from grinding poverty due to the power of economic growth. The knowledge and tools bequeathed by the Scientific Revolution marked a paradigm shift in our relationship with the physical and natural world. With the scientific method of experimentation, rational deduction and mathematical description, natural laws took the place of divine intervention, and enabled an entirely new understanding of and mastery over nature. The Scientific Revolution was accompanied by the great European voyages of discovery and the emergence, for the first time in human history, of our knowledge of the true geographical extent of the world.

The discoveries of science and global exploration undermined the dogmatic certainties of church and monarchy, providing an antidote to the violent oppression of religion in Mediaeval Europe, with its inquisitions, witch burnings, and brutal sectarian wars. During the seventeenth and eighteenth centuries, the ideas of the Enlightenment, of individual liberty, progress, and representative government laid the foundations for democracy and equality and hope for our emergence from the long age of tyranny.

The nineteenth century built on the progress of previous centuries as the Industrial Revolution unleashed the material resources needed to enable humanity's escape from poverty and disease. During the 2000 years separating ancient Greece from seventeenth-century Europe, living standards around the world had barely changed and sheer survival remained the overriding concern for the majority of humanity. The Industrial Revolution, by contrast, fuelled what economist Angus Deaton has called humanity's Great Escape from deprivation. Through the creation of a vast range of industries, from trains, shipping, automotive, aviation, chemicals, pharmaceuticals, defence, communications and computing, the proportion of the world's population in extreme poverty fell from 84% prior to the Industrial Revolution to below 25% today. The benefits of economic development have not been spread evenly, of course, with a minority of rich countries

DOI: 10.4324/9781003376811-6

benefitting most. But in recent decades, even this wealth gap has begun to close, as economic development in China and India have raised more than one billion people out of extreme poverty.

In this telling, modernity has been a story of miraculous progress on many fronts. Science has brought us a profoundly different understanding of our place in the cosmos, medicine has vastly improved our health and longevity, material progress has provided a level of affluence for the majority of humanity that was previously the preserve of nobility, democracy has become the dominant form of government, a global system of human rights law exists to enforce principles of equality for all, and the principle of tolerance, whereby "patient and unprejudiced endurance of dissent from the generally received cause or view", has become the standard of the modern age (Van Loon, 1927).

Alongside this first tale of modernity, however, lies a second, very different, tale. This tale acknowledges that deep pathologies lie within modernity which are conveniently omitted in the first telling. In this telling, progress has come at tremendous cost and has been based largely on violence, exclusion, and destruction.

This tale acknowledges that the prosperity of the developed world resulted from a process of colonisation driven by barbarity and genocide. To cite just one example from Christopher Columbus' celebrated 'discovery' of the Americas: Columbus "massed together several hundred armoured troops, cavalry and a score or more of trained attack dogs. They set forth across the countryside, tearing into assembled masses of sick and unarmed native people, slaughtering them by the thousands" (Stannard, 1993:69). The great European voyages of discovery unleashed centuries of such wanton violence and genocide around the globe.

This second tale of modernity acknowledges that modernity was built upon and remains imbued with racism, sexism, and hypermasculinity. The colonial system which the European powers constructed had as its primary purpose the extraction, by force, of material wealth from the colonies. The slave trade and oppression of native peoples, which were justified on the basis of the sub-human nature of non-white peoples, were the essential foundations of modernity. In such a brutal system, not only were 'inferior' women unsuited to positions of authority. So too were men who did not display the violent, aggressive hypermasculinity necessary to oversee and maintain such a cruel, violent order.

This second tale of modernity also acknowledges that capitalism, along with the undoubted benefits it has brought, has also fundamentally altered humanity's concept of value. Money and material possessions have become the new arbiter of human worth and the horizon by which human lives should be guided. Two quotes illustrate the nature of this profound transition. A leading advocate for the 'Americanisation' of native Americans, writing in 1896, set out the task at hand:

> To bring him out of savagery into citizenship... we need to awaken in him wants. In his dull savagery he must be touched by the wings of the divine angel of discontent... Discontent with the tepee and the starving rations of the

Indian camp in winter is needed to get the Indian out of the blanket and into trousers – and trousers with a pocket in them, and with a pocket that aches to be filled with dollars.

(Ghosh, 2021:174)

The founder of economics, Adam Smith, acknowledged the importance of envy in modern capitalism when he wrote that wealth is "desired not for the material satisfactions that it brings but because it is desired by others". Modernity is designed to engender an aching and insatiable desire for material wealth based not on needs but on envy.

This tale also acknowledges that the modern idea of mastery over nature has brought upon us impending environmental catastrophe and the existential threat of climate change. As Amitav Ghosh emphasises, the 'de-sacralisation' of Nature was one of the key battlegrounds of modernity. To be 'civilised' was to accept the idea that the Earth is inert and machine-like, just as Newton told us. A defining feature of the 'savagery' of native peoples was their belief in the vitality and 'sacredness' of nature, a 'savagery' which was extinguished through the barrel of the gun. Modernity today denigrates the myth, mystery, mysticism, and enchantment of the pre-modern worldview, and still dismisses the value of subjectivity and art as ways of seeing the entirety of reality (Byrne, 2021).

This second tale of modernity therefore, while accepting the blessings it has brought, recognises modernity as a historic construction, the product of centuries of combined Western effort going back to the 1500s, which contains within it deep pathologies of the past. And it is on these pathologies that violent disordered leaders, past and present, have risen to power.

Strongmen Leaders and the Strengths and Pathologies of Modernity

The early twenty-first century has been marked by the rise of strongman leaders around the world intent on destroying the positives of modernity and strengthening its pathologies. The world's two most populous countries, China and India, have come under the rule of autocratic leaders in the persons of Xi Jinping and Narendra Modi. Under Xi, power in China has been consolidated in the hands of a single individual in ways not seen since the death of Mao. Under Modi, India has been pursuing a form of sectarian Hindu nationalism that vilifies the country's large Muslim minority. In Brazil, Jair Bolsonaro led an assault on state institutions, vilifying indigenous peoples, and assaulting the environment. In the United States, Donald Trump's assault on democracy culminated in the incitement of a violent assault on the US Capitol Building in an attempt to halt the transfer of power to newly elected President Joe Biden. In Russia, Vladimir Putin has dismantled democracy, established one of the world's richest kleptocracies, eliminated free speech, established a pattern of assassinating opponents, and led Russia to a state of almost constant warfare, culminating in the barbarous invasion of Ukraine. In short, Putin has destroyed the four positives of modernity – science and reason, tolerance of dissent, human rights and equality, and accountable democratic government. And he has built his power on modernity's three core pathologies – violence; materialism and greed; and inequalities based on a hypermasculinity which denigrates love and care.

Destroying the Four Positives

Science and Reason

The idea that truth exists and that it can be found on the basis of evidence and reasoned argument is a central pillar of modernity. Science and reason eroded the authoritarian power of popes and kings, as facts and evidence replaced edicts from unchallenged autocrats as the basis of shared reality. Today's authoritarian leaders, however, wish to return to a time when truth is what they say it is and facts are simply a matter of opinion. Putin stands as the archetype among today's strongman leaders in establishing such a post-truth world. Whereas twentieth-century totalitarian leaders sought to impose rigid ideologies – of communism or National Socialism – as the unquestionable truth, the current wave of strongman rulers place less emphasis on ideology. Instead, they aim to create a fog of confusion, based on endless torrents of lies, conspiracy theories, denials, and false hints and accusations. This deliberate strategy aims to undermine all sources of information and destroy the very concept of facts and truth. In such a society, where the foundations of shared reality have been destroyed and where people do not know what is true anymore, reasoned opposition and holding leaders to account becomes impossible. In today's Russia, Putin has created an all-embracing dis-information ecosystem whereby every information source, from Putin to politicians, state media, television news, and social media, all traffic in lies and conspiracies. As Peter Pomerantsev has written, what is increasingly becoming the world's post-truth future, under Putin, arrived in Russia first (Pomerantsev, 2019).

Tolerance of Dissent

A second pillar of modernity is tolerance of dissent. The struggle for freedom to think, speak and act on the basis of individual conscience, in so far as this does not cause harm to others, is central in the narrative of modernity. The history of modernity tells of a long line of courageous martyrs who were willing to speak the truth regardless of the consequences, from Galileo's defiance of the church to Martin Luther King's challenge to white supremacy. Such freedoms are the basis of progress, both in science and in society, where the ability to question established ideas and practices is essential if new and better ways of living and understanding are to be found. Russian dissidents take their place in this long history, of course, from Alexandr Solzhenitsyn to Andrei Sakharov to Alexei Navalny. Putin, and other contemporary strongman leaders, demolish this pillar of modernity by brutally silencing dissent.

Equality and Human Rights

The principle of equality – that one person's worth is the same as every other – forms yet another pillar of modernity. The history of humanity clearly illustrates our propensity for finding ways to denigrate, subjugate, and eliminate others, on the basis of sex, skin colour, nationality, sexual orientation, and disability. One of the most hopeful narratives within modernity is of our progress in overcoming this appalling characteristic of our species. Modernity has succeeded, however imperfectly, in establishing norms of equality that are unprecedented in history. Once again, Putin and other strongman leaders seek to halt and reverse this process. In Putin's Russia, rights for women and sexual minorities have been reversed. Domestic violence in Russia, for example, is not a criminal offence provided it does not result in hospitalisation. Homophobic campaigns on state media deride LGBTQ+ people as perverts, sodomites, and abnormal, and conflate homosexuality with paedophilia. And in Ukraine, Putin seeks to resurrect the colonial idea of 'inferior peoples' in his vilification of the entire Ukrainian population as 'Nazis' and subhuman.

Accountable Democratic Government

A fourth pillar of modernity that authoritarian leaders seek to destroy is democracy. And from their perspective, with good reason. Democracy is an extensive system of defences against autocratic rule. This system comprises the rule of law, which applies equally to leaders as to citizens; it includes a system of checks and balances on power, including a democratically elected parliament, opposition parties, and a constitution which no leader can transgress; it includes the separation of church and state, to prevent leaders from allying themselves with the power of the religious establishment; and it includes a system of legal protections for individual rights and freedoms, including the freedom to dissent. Since each of these components of democracy place limits on the power of leaders, autocrats invariably seek to dismantle them once they attain power. This too is true in the case of Putin. Power in Russia is concentrated in Putin's hands, elections are manipulated, parliament is neutered, the judiciary is subservient, the media is under state control, and extra-judicial arrests and assassinations to silence dissent are common.

Valorising the Three Pathologies

Violence

Let us turn now to the pathologies of modernity. Unfortunately, what Walter Wink has called the myth of redemptive violence was one of the founding pillars of modernity and remains deeply embedded within it to this day (Wink, 1999). The myth of redemptive violence is the belief that violence saves, that war brings peace, that 'might makes right'. It is one of the oldest continuously repeated stories in the world. Modernity has sought to replace this rule by force with the rule of law. Today's rule-based international order – however imperfect – with its institutions

Vladimir Putin and the Pathologies of Modernity 97

and norms of negotiation and diplomacy seeks to protect sovereignty, particularly of smaller states, and preserve peace by curbing the excessive use of force. The alternative to this rule-based system is a world of all-against-all, where violence determines the hierarchy of power among states. It is to such a violent zeitgeist that strongman leaders wish to return. The dynamic of militarism and violence favours men with a very specific psychology – namely the violent, the aggressive, the ruthlessly ambitious and the pathologically narcissistic, those without conscience (Hughes, 2018). Putin, violent to his core, has built his power on his language of denigration, threat, and abuse, on his murderous elimination of opponents, and on his barbarous wars. Up until his failed invasion of Ukraine, he demonstrated at each step, to himself and the world, that violence does pay.

Materialism and Compulsive Greed

Next to violence, unbridled greed is the most conspicuous characteristic of the strongman leader. So common is this shared characteristic that it has given its name to the type of government that such leaders create – kleptocracy. Kleptocracy is the term used to describe 'government by thieves', whereby political elites systematically raid state resources to enrich themselves and their families. Kleptocracy is enabled by the absence of democratic checks and balances on those in power. To create such conditions, kleptocratic leaders systematically undermine the rule of law, subjugate the courts and media, and deploy state security services to enrich themselves and pacify the population. Alexei Navalny has highlighted Putin's obsession with material wealth and indeed describes Putin's regime as one of 'crooks and thieves'. Navalny famously exposed Putin's Palace, a sprawling billion-dollar palace situated on a hilltop overlooking the Black Sea, which allegedly includes a Japanese garden, a marble gym, a full-size theatre, a casino, a church, and an ice hockey arena. The fortunes amassed by Putin and his inner circle are such that Russia leads the world in terms of the amount of wealth hidden in offshore tax havens, both in terms of absolute volume – estimates placed it around $800 billion in 2017 – and as a percentage of national GDP.

Hypermasculinity

A third pathology that modernity struggles to overcome, but which remains deeply embedded within it, is hypermasculinity. Masculine domination is one of the most universal and enduring features of human societies, stretching back to the very advent of the state. From its origins millennia ago, the state has been predominantly the purview of male God-Kings, emperors, sultans, presidents, and prime ministers. Modernity, with its principles of equality between men and women, and diplomacy in the place of violence, seeks to end this long night of hypermasculine domination. The dominance of aggressive hypermasculinity has consequences both for men and women. Aggressive narcissistic males assert their power and assume leadership by ridiculing and debasing other forms of masculinity. This 'war within masculinity' targets men who exhibit 'feminine' qualities of empathy, respect and care, intellectual curiosity, 'deviant' sexuality (gay men), and weakness (disabled men, poor men). The consequences for women are even more destructive. The division of labour, and the value ascribed to tasks in society, are apportioned on the basis of a hypermasculine value system whose circularity defines whatever is done by hypermasculine males as highly valuable, and whatever is done by women as being inherently of less value. As a result, the very functions which are essential to the survival of humanity – producing and nurturing life – are denigrated and devalued. In their place, violence, militarism, aggression, and materialism are valorised and rewarded. Such is clearly the case at present in Putin's hypermasculine Russia.

The Metamorphosis of Modernity – Containing Pathological Leaders

Sociologist Ulrich Beck calls modernity a kind of compulsive collective memory in that it contains within it our past decisions and mistakes (Beck, 2016). These mistakes, moreover, are now confronting us with existential crises, including climate change, the biodiversity crisis, environmental degradation, and nuclear weapons, that present themselves as objectified threats to our existence. The strengthening of the pathologies of modernity – militarism, compulsive greed, excessive materialism, and violent hypermasculinity – and the erosion of its positives – tolerance, equality, human rights, objective truth, and democracy – are now threatening our very existence. Pathological leaders, like Vladimir Putin, are driving us to destruction.

Under these conditions, Beck argues, a fundamental reformation of institutions – of politics, economics, gender, technology, education – is now "urgent, morally imperative and politically possible". In fact, he argues, it is already underway. This metamorphosis is questioning the pathologies of modernity and seeking positive responses to the deep crises we are confronted by. This process is not a consciously intended, programmatic change in society. It is not a deterministic process whose end is pre-ordained. As Beck warns, it could lead to catastrophe, but there is scope too for that he calls "emancipatory catastrophism" – the possibility that impending catastrophe could make changes possible that seem impossible today.

In fact, emancipatory catastrophism has been the driving force in the development of democracy. As I have argued elsewhere, the primary purpose of democracy is to safeguard society against the devastation that people with dangerous disorders – such as Hitler, Mao, Stalin, and Putin – cause when they come to power (Hughes, 2018).

From this psychological perspective, our system of liberal representative democracy was constructed piece by piece by those who went before us, often in the aftermath of war and genocide, to protect against the destructiveness of a dangerous minority. This dangerous minority is comprised of those who suffer from a range of personality disorders – narcissistic personality disorder, paranoid personality

Vladimir Putin and the Pathologies of Modernity 99

disorder, and psychopathy – which render them incapable of empathy or conscience. While the scientific evidence for the existence and prevalence of dangerous disorders was not available to the ancient Athenians, the Founding Fathers of the US Constitution, or the signatories to the Universal Declaration of Human Rights, the destructive consequences of this minority were painfully evident to them all. Without describing what they were doing in the language of psychology, the architects of liberal democracy were nevertheless constructing a defensive system to protect against psychologically disordered leaders and their followers. Through conflict after conflict, the democrats of previous generations created the pillars that make up our modern system of liberal representative democracy – the rule of law, free and fair elections, the separation of church and state, social democracy and the welfare state, legal protection for human rights, shared sovereignty in international institutions, and cultures of tolerance.

Every one of these pillars of democracy arose in response to catastrophes that dangerous personalities wrought. What was previously impossible became reality in the form of new institutions, values, and ways of living that sought to contain pathological leaders and create conditions for greater human flourishing.

Today, modernity's successes are exposing and confronting its pathologies. The positives within the contemporary process of metamorphosis are enabling waves of emancipation on issues ranging from sex equality, hypermasculinity, racism, and nationalism. But such fundamental change is also creating a backlash. It is upon this backlash that today's wave of strongmen have come to power, with Putin as their archetype. Putin is a KGB man who believes deeply in the oppressive worldview of the Soviet Union – that the West is the enemy and is intent on destroying Russia, that dissent is traitorous and must be silenced. He specialises in the KGB methods of assassination, disinformation, and paranoia. A violent vindictive man with a closed mind, he embodies a toxic combination of paranoid imperialism, corruption and self-enrichment, and hatred of democracy. Putin is a destroyer of the positives of modernity and defender of its pathologies.

But Putin's blatant pathology provides an opportunity for change. Leaders with dangerously disordered minds have always posed a threat to society, as evidenced by the calamities of twentieth century caused by Stalin, Hitler, and Mao, among many others. Today, in the face of climate change and nuclear weapons, that threat is global, immediate, and existential. As Beck highlights, however, this moment of extreme danger is also a moment of potential transformation – of metamorphosis. We have the possibility – and the moral obligation – to steward a transformation in modernity that will mitigate the threat from leaders with dangerously disordered minds, address the cascading crises we face, and create the foundations for the next, and better, phase of human history.

A new narrative of modernity is necessary for human survival. The outlines of this narrative are already clear. It is a narrative that draws together the great threads of history – of human equality, of peace and non-violence, of love and care as pre-conditions for our survival, and of democracy as our defence against pathology. It is a narrative of humility in which we acknowledge our mutual dependence on each other as equals (Ghosh, 2021); in which the radical discontinuity between humans and nature is overcome (Berry, 2011); and in which each of us are called to play our part through the ways we live our lives (Ressa, 2022). Most importantly, it is a narrative in which Putin and his fellow disordered minds are written out.

References

Beck, U. (2016). *The metamorphosis of the world: How climate change is transforming our concept of the world*. John Wiley & Sons.

Berry, T. (2011). *The great work: Our way into the future*. Crown.

Byrne, E. (2021). Why the metaphor of complementary dualism, and metaphor itself, are foundational to achieving sustainability. In *Metaphor, sustainability, transformation* (pp. 119–136). Routledge. Ian Hughes, Edmond Byrne, Gerard Mullally, Colin Sage.

Ghosh, A. (2021). *The nutmeg's curse*. University of Chicago Press.

Hughes, I. (2018). *Disordered minds: How dangerous personalities are destroying democracy*. John Hunt Publishing.

Pomerantsev, P. (2019). *This is not propaganda: Adventures in the war against reality*. PublicAffairs.

Ressa, M. (2022). *How to stand up to a dictator: The fight for our future*. Penguin.

Stannard, D. E. (1993). *American holocaust: The conquest of the new world*. Oxford University Press.

Van Loon, H. W. (1927). *Tolerance: Hendrik Van Loon*. Boni et Liveright.

Wink, W. (1999). *The powers that be: Theology for a new millennium*. Harmony.

Chapter 7

Nuclear Blackmail

James R. Merikangas

In the first part of the twentieth century, two similar nations, separated by language and the River Rhine, fought from forests and trenches killing about ten million soldiers and about ten million civilians. Another 20 million were wounded before a fragile peace and much poverty ensued. It is still unclear why this happened, and historians argue, and philosophers still speculate, but the trajectory to another wider war had been launched almost from the signing of the Treaty of Versailles. An obscure enlisted man from that war, Adolph Hitler, rode the wave of shame and resentment, prejudice, and bigotry, to build a massive war machine employing a disciplined and indoctrinated citizenry in an attempt to establish an empire (the 3rd Reich) and to take back what he thought was his to claim. Thinly veiled excuses for simple aggression and theft justified the most terrible crimes and aggression. Appropriation of land and resources were excused with racial and cultural hatred and given license by political and community support. It was against this background of unspeakable murders that war changed from contests between soldiers on the battlefield to mass murder of civilians in their homes. The bombings of London by German airplanes and V-2 missiles were meant to terrorize populations rather than to paralyze the production and transport of men and material for battle. Whether in reciprocity or reprisal, the British and Americans began the bombing of cities, including the incineration of Dresden, a cultural center of no strategic importance, and the firebombing of Tokyo, the most destructive bombing raid in history. As World War I turned out to not be "the war to end wars", the denouement of World War II in the Pacific was the beginning of the Atomic Age with the nuclear incineration of Hiroshima and Nagasaki. For a while the United States of America was invincible, but then Russia exploded their own atomic bomb on August 29, 1949. Thus began the Cold War and era of "mutually assured destruction" that maintained a type of uneasy peace with the knowledge an attack on one nuclear power by another would result in not only it's destruction, but the destruction of the aggressor in an unstoppable counterattack. This doomsday scenario hovered over the national psyche for many years. Testing of atomic bombs and the massively more destructive hydrogen bombs were undertaken both above ground and underground while the arsenals of the USA, the Soviet Union, and later China, Israel, Great Britain, France, India, Pakistan, North Korea, and perhaps some others

DOI: 10.4324/9781003376811-7

stored thousands of bombs that could be dropped from aircraft, launched from submarines or silos, and made small enough to be fired from howitzers or drones. The smaller "tactical" weapons can be as powerful as those that incinerated Hiroshima and Nagasaki, and there can be no effective defense from them. A freighter or cruise ship could sail into New York City harbor and kill ten million people with no warning and with no certain origin. Such an attack would likely trigger massive retaliation that would end civilization and make the earth uninhabitable. All life that did not die instantly, except perhaps for fish and insects, would die slowly from persisting radiation poisoning.

On July 9, 1962, I stood on the flight deck of the aircraft carrier USS *Kitty Hawk* and witnessed the last above ground explosion of a hydrogen bomb, Operation Starfish Prime. An explosion equivalent to 1.5 million tons of TNT was detonated 250 miles above Johnson Island in the Pacific, causing a 90-minute aurora illuminating the night from horizon to horizon and knocking out radio communication as far away as Hawaii. There was no sound, as the explosion was above the atmosphere in outer space. In October 1962, I was in the Formosa Straits (now Taiwan) with our jet bombers on the flight deck of our ship loaded with nuclear bombs and with pilots in the cockpits ready to launch on order to strike China. We of course did not know why this was happening, before the internet and news outlets on TV, but we were ready to kill millions of innocent people because they were communists. Although I had attended the Navy Guided Missile School and the nuclear weapons loading course, I decided to leave the service and go to medical school, moving from mass destruction to individual healing. Despite studying medicine and human behavior and becoming a neuropsychiatrist I remain unable to explain the psychopathology of Napoleon, Hitler, Stalin, and Putin, except as a mixture of paranoia, narcissism, and psychopathy. Any use of nuclear weapons, even "tactical" ones, would amount to suicide.

The United States after winning the war in Europe did the unprecedented act of not appropriating real estate and resources, of not enslaving the German population, but rather through the brilliant device of the Marshall Plan helped to rebuild the devastation of bombed out cities and factories, thus leading to the European democracies as we know them today. This was, however, against the competing force of communism in Russia and Eastern Europe under Russian domination. Again, for reasons of ideology, greed, envy, and any list of human failings, the victors in World War II became competitors instead of partners and deadly opponents in the "Cold War".

After a few local wars in Korea, Vietnam, Iraq, Syria, Libya, and the continuing war and occupation of the former Palestine, we have not had serious threats of nuclear annihilation until now. From the age of ***mutually assured destruction***, we now have entered the era of ***nuclear blackmail***. Vladimir Putin has invaded Ukraine and threatened to use tactical nuclear weapons if there is retaliation against Russia itself or if the Ukrainians continue to resist annexation. This threat of first use of nuclear weapons is dangerous and irrational. To allow a nuclear armed country to get its way because of such a threat is the very definition of blackmail. The use of "conventional" weapons to control and dominate no longer requires victory, because when the aggressor begins to lose, the use of a threat of nuclear war is expected to make the defense back down and give up because the alternative is a nuclear explosion killing thousands and rendering the land uninhabitable for a thousand years. One might think that only a madman, a suicidal psychopath, would choose death over defeat. We have, however, many examples of suicide bombers, Kamikaze pilots, religious martyrs, and others not considered psychotic, choosing to die for their convictions. We have no consensus on when religious faith becomes delusional, or when patriotism becomes fanatical. There may be agreement that invading a sovereign country is morally wrong, and that Hitler and Putin were not justified in aggression, but was the "shock and Awe" bombing of Baghdad justified? There is a fine line, or blurred border, between religious faith, overvalued belief, and psychotic delusion. Failing a personal interview and a neurological examination, I cannot determine what form of pathology afflicts Vladimir Putin.

There are more than 800 books written about Adolf Hitler, including the famous analysis by Walter Langer for the OSS in 1943, and the one by Fritz Redlich, a former Dean of Yale Medical School, that attempt to understand his psychopathology. Although they make interesting reading, something is left lacking. Redlich concluded Hitler was simply EVIL, Langer correctly predicted Hitler's suicide, but we lack similar studies of Putin. My reading of Hitler's history suggests his personality disorder and subsequent deterioration to Parkinson's disease may have been the result of the episode of measles he had when he was about 12 years old. Measles always goes to the brain, and when it causes encephalitis, the child may die or be left with permanent neurological damage, including a lack of empathy and psychopathic traits. Hitler was reportedly a normal child until he had measles, and underwent a personality change thereafter. Because of mass vaccination many doctors are unaware of this complication as a sequel of measles, but it can happen with any virus, as exhibited by the massive increase in Parkinson's disease after the famous Spanish Flu. We have yet to see the end result of *Long Covid,* but I would not be surprised to see an increase in antisocial behavior. We have seen a decrease in crime and ADHD as lead has been removed from gasoline and the environment. This epidemiological observation demonstrates the importance of brain damage and low IQ in the etiology of crime but is not sufficiently publicized along with the sociological and cultural arguments commonly seen. We can only guess what Putin's childhood was like, because he has spent so much energy burnishing his image as a macho martial arts fighter and brilliant politician that one forgets that he is only 5'6" tall and 70 years old.

Using *Nuclear Blackmail* to shield the slaughter of civilians in an unprovoked invasion of a neighboring country is certainly the work of a person lacking a conscience. To do something because you can get away with it is a human trait we have seen throughout history. The Abrahamic religions, whether Jew, Muslim, or Christian, teach charity and compassion toward strangers, but have nevertheless failed to prevent conquest, slaughter, persecution, and crime. Charismatic figures, either political or religious, will continue to dominate world events until the scientific understanding of the brain melds neurobiology with psychology and shapes child development and educational policy. The study of figures like Napoleon, Stalin, Hitler, and Putin, remains important if civilization is to survive the nuclear age.

Summary

Richard Wood

There was an overall agreement that Putin is a profoundly destructive leader. Some of us focused upon his pursuit of the wars that he has initiated or participated in (Syria, Chechnya, Georgia, and Ukraine) and/or his suppression of critical democratic institutions (like the Free Press, the Duma, and the judiciary), noting that his efforts to fulfil these ambitions has been marked by striking brutality, tenacity, and ruthlessness that seems to have typified him since the inception of his presidencies. People who have opposed him have lost their lives, been jailed, or exiled. The biographical sources that many of us relied upon extensively documented violations of the electoral process, of the Russian Constitution, and his dedication to misinformation. All of our writers, in one form or another, were deeply distressed by his lack of humanity and lack of regard for others' lives, dignity, needs for safety, and voice. Wood also expressed deep anxiety about a strategic vision that seems to embrace weaponization of refugees, economies, energy, and food as a means of enhancing populist movements and destabilizing democracies.

Virtually all of us felt that there was a great deal we couldn't know about what his childhood was like. Some of us (Willock and Wood) believed that it was reasonable to work with the limited biographical data that we had about his childhood, augmenting our understanding of it by working back in time, relying on the shape that his adult personality has assumed to help us make better sense of how various aspects of his childhood might have impacted him. There is, in fact, extensive biographical information about his adult behaviour and relationships. Working backwards in such a manner is a familiar pathway that one follows in one's work with patients, adhering to a standard method that focuses first upon observable defences, then identification of the anxiety driving them, and, finally, upon articulation of core conflicts that one can either surmise or, sometimes, in the context of a treatment relationship, observe directly. The standard method implicitly relies upon concepts like repetition compulsion and traumatic re-enactment; that is, one expects that deeply painful traumatic experiences will seek to re-express themselves in a variety of ways in an adult personality.

Wood also used his understanding of the working model of malignant narcissism he had constructed to help guide him through this process while Willock relied upon Guntrip's appraisal of schizoid personality to do the same. Willock also

DOI: 10.4324/9781003376811-8

brought the concepts of multiple dissociative self states, intergenerational trauma, and adverse childhood experience (ACE) to an understanding of the trauma that Putin likely experienced. He ventured into facets of Putin's early years that many biographers have discredited but which, in the context of his description of these events, seemed to offer potentially important explanations of Putin's attachment history. We are referring here to Willock's exposition of one theory about Putin's parentage that maintains that his biological mother was actually a Georgian woman who had Putin out of wedlock, not the woman that Putin has always identified as his birthmother whom he says delivered him when she was 41 years old. While biographers have generally discredited this Georgian possibility, the wealth of detail which Willock reviews supporting this story does give one pause. If, indeed, the alternate pathway that Willock describes was Putin's actuality, it would mean that during the first ten years of his life, he was moved through a variety of different caretakers and placements before finally settling in the apartment on Baskov Lane with the people that he publicly endorses as his parents. The scenario that Willock outlines might argue that Putin was subject to multiple rejections and broken attachments before finally being afforded a stable home. In private communication, Willock and Wood both considered that such a growing-up experience might conceivably produce the kind of attachment disorder that one so frequently sees working with foster children. Such children face profound obstacles in their attempts to trust others and to develop deep, meaningful, mutually satisfying interdependencies. At this point in time, however, one has no definitive way of knowing which origin story is accurate. Accordingly, even though these comments have to be treated as suppositional, one would venture that they are deserving of further examination of the data and additional analysis before they can be dismissed.

Though Willock and Wood explored different pathways (schizoid versus malignant narcissism) that Putin might have moved through as he became the person that he is, their appreciation of both some of the core dynamics that they believed typified Putin and their grasp of the kind of deficits that such dynamics were likely to have produced was in many respects similar. Putin was seen to have surrendered foundational parts of his humanity – much of his capacity to love and be loved and to empathize with others – in response to traumatizing experiences that served to push him into an increasingly solipsistic existence. Both authors also saw Putin as struggling with a devastated, frightening inner world populated with both threatening representations of the self and of others. In order to escape the persecutory threat that such an inner world creates, Putin could be seen to have adopted a persecutory stance meant to protect him from the bad objects that had piled up inside, becoming an aggressor rather than a victim. In both of these scenarios (schizoid personality and malignant narcissism), ruptured attachments could conceivably have played a very important role in shaping Putin, but so, too, might have the trauma of the courtyard, particularly in a context in which parents were ill-equipped, by virtue of their preoccupation with their own devastating past, to be able to attend to his needs in a sensitive and supportive fashion. Still, the differences between a schizoid

Summary 107

formulation and malignant narcissistic one remained substantial. Both Willock and Wood recognized that their ideas were propositional. Both look forward to more extended conversations with colleagues who hopefully might offer additional diagnostic perspectives. Willock, following Guntrip, invited and promoted discussion of how underlying schizoid processes, malignant narcissism, and psychopathy can go hand in hand in character (de)formation.

Coline Covington saw Putin as a leader who replaced ideology – which was defining for the Russians of the communist regime – with the mythology of Russianness and Eurasian identity that stipulates that Russians are essentially innocent and that Russian culture will inevitably express itself in the ways that it must, including acts of aggression against perceived enemies. She characterized this mythology by the term that Putin had used: "passionarnost" – a conception that, as she described it, almost sounded like Darwinian justification. Passionarnost was natural, reflected the will of the sociocultural body being described, was instinctual, was not a matter of choice or policy, entailed suffering to protect national identity, and inherently sought to pursue growth and expansion. She also referenced Timothy Snyder's ideas of inevitability and eternity, considering that Putin had moved Russia into an atmosphere of eternity, which could be described as one in which external enemies are seen to continuously assault and jeopardize the mother country. Putin had accomplished this end by reminding the Russian people of their "chosen traumas" and "chosen glories" and by raising false flags about perceived enemies who meant to harm Russia and the ethos of the Russian spirit. Chosen traumas that she saw Putin invoking included the Mongol invasions of the thirteenth century, Napoleon's invasion in the early nineteenth century, and of course the great patriotic war. Identifying himself as the "saviour" who could protect Mother Russia against an essentially hostile world, Putin both consolidated his own authority and affirmed the innocence of the Russian people, whom he defined through their victimhood. In a telling passage, she further commented that:

> it is apparent that Putin is provoking the West to retaliate in order to further justify (his) position of being the besieged country. This is the classic position of the bully who gains power by accusing his opponent of being the bully.
>
> (p. 8)

The dynamic that Covington describes could be seen to be a classic example of projective identification or its blame-shifting alter ego, depending upon how conscious one thinks Putin is of the manoeuvres he carries out. It is reminiscent of the position Dennis the Menace took with his father when, facing questioning about his behaviour, Dennis replied, "it all started when he hit me back."

At the very end of her chapter, Covington warned that "there is no limit to Putin's resolve to protect Russia, even if it means that Russia goes down with the rest of the world," citing Homer-Dixon (2022). Like Wood, she referenced the "suicidal end of Hitler's Reich," asking us to remember that while such a position is obviously irrational, our expectation that Putin would not be compelled by irrationality "fails to recognize the insanity of collective innocence and the danger it poses to us all."

(p. 77)

Covington and Wood also commented on the nature of the leader-follower relationship.

Covington felt the great mass of the Russian people could indeed be characterized as "innocent," at least in the sense that the endless, voluminous barrage of state misinformation puts them in a position of not being able to know, to judge, and to act (one could also add, to feel). In the face of such ambiguity and uncertainty, she also argued that people are inclined to become apathetic and to experience loss of agency. Without agency, people cannot reflect upon the state's actions, and without the capacity for reflection, we have no moral compass, as Covington notes Hannah Arendt has suggested. In the context of overall mistrust in the media, people rely upon their sense of national identity to help them resolve questions of what is moral and what is not. In that sense, misinformation and a stream of contradictory views represents a deliberate strategy that autocrats can employ to further consolidate control. Her ideas, while counterintuitive, strike one as deeply perceptive.

She also strongly cautioned those outside the Russian environment need to sidestep any inclination we might feel to villainize the Russian population as a whole. Such an approach to our view of the Russian people, she argued, represented an archaic form of thinking growing out of our need, especially when we are very afraid, to see people as either all good or all bad. She was also deeply concerned about the ease with which the devout innocence of the Russian mass could transform itself into dangerous paranoia, implicitly underscoring the readiness which not being able to know could mutate into profound, dangerous mistrust. While she did not say so explicitly, she seemed to be telling us that such mistrust could be readily harnessed to serve the pathological aims of an autocratic leader. She cited the Serbian scholar, Dzihic, who posited that disinformation "throws dust in the eyes of the public" and can thereby enhance the group's subservience to an autocratic leader (quoted NYR Daily, The Age of Total Lies, V. Pesic and C. Cimic, 6/2/17).

Like many other authors, Wood acknowledged that real and perceived society-wide injuries and disruptions that could be occasioned by experiences like war and severe economic privation helped lay the ground for receptivity to an autocratic presence. In his consideration of the leader-follower relationship, Wood enumerated a number of dynamics that potentially render an autocratic leader nearly irresistible to those he would govern. Projection of obdurate strength and certainty; manufactured crises that may exacerbate threat in an already humiliated and alienated population; leader capacity to attune himself and to align himself with the sense of fear and narcissistic injury a given population has endured (creating an illusion of empathic attunement and a shared sense of alienation on the part of leader and follower); opportunity to participate in and partake of the leader's sense of personal aggrandizement and omnipotence; people's discomfort with their own seemingly chaotic, ungovernable inner worlds, creating willingness to embrace someone else's moral authority; people's need to join with a strong other (perhaps because they struggle with a chronic, formidable sense of incompleteness); people's hunger for sense of community, purpose, and meaning; culturally inculcated authoritarian personality in the wider population that hobbles people's ability to think independently; and people's relative lack of self-awareness were all fell to make their own potential contribution to this vulnerability.

The costs of participating in such a "Faustian" bargain were seen to be high. Such costs included absorbing the autocrat's endemic, pervasive levels of fear into their own lives; learning, as a means of procuring safety in a fear-drenched environment, to bully others lower in the autocratic hierarchies that surround them; being prepared, again as a means of procuring safety, to direct rage and humiliation towards those whom the state has decided to hate; accommodating themselves to nearly unendurably high levels of hypervigilance, reflective of the autocrat's investment in a war footing stance; loss of the capacity to feel and to be human as their own interiors are increasingly defined by the dark impulses and acts that they must accommodate themselves to; diminishment of their capacity for reason and nuanced thought informed by empathy; and increasing movement towards the psychopathic existence that defines the autocrat. If the autocratic leader has initiated a war or series of wars, society as a whole must somehow absorb the guilt and shame that hideous acts of war inevitably occasion into their already ravaged souls. Acts of cruelty and rapacity become the means through which people can confirm their potency and aliveness rather than acts of love and decency. Wood argued that the autocrat's impact on those that he governs is a reflection of deep, implacable envy of other's humanity – humanity that he himself can never experience in a meaningful way.

Ian Hughes provides us with a meaningful, critical overview of the course of human history, reminding us that the forces of modernity that have helped relieve some sectors of humanity from the bondage of poverty and the subjugation of autocratic leadership have also contained within them potent, destructive forces which now jeopardize us. Those forces have included valorization of racism, sexism, and hypermasculinity side-by-side our investment in a version of capitalism that monetizes human value and elevates envy as a human virtue. It also invites us to think of the earth as "inert and machinelike" rather than as a vulnerable, organic entity deserving of our respect. Hughes cites Byrne's (2021) appraisal that "modernity today denigrates the myth, mystery, mysticism, and enchantment of the premodern worldview, and still dismisses the value of subjectivity and art as ways of seeing the entirety of reality."

Hughes tells us that the destructive forces of modernity have helped set the stage for the rise of strongmen leaders like Trump, Modi, Bolsonaro, and Putin. He also believes that the fundamental, positive changes embedded in modernity have created a backlash upon which "today's wave of strongmen have come to power ..." – a position that Wood would very much endorse. Hughes sees Putin's erosion of the "four positives" of modernity (science and reason, tolerance of dissent, equality and human rights, and accountable democratic government) as archetypal, documenting the variety of ways in which Putin has systematically destroyed modernity's greatest assets, replacing them instead with valorization of violence, materialism and compulsive greed, and reinvestment in hypermasculine values that is causing a war within masculinity (targeting men who exhibit feminine qualities of empathy, respect and care, intellectual curiosity, deviant sexuality, and weakness). The arguments that he makes about Putin's attack on truth, replacing it with disinformation, echo dynamics Covington has outlined in her chapter in this book.

Hughes sees Beck's concept of emancipatory catastrophism (Beck, 2016) as a means through which humanity might find its way towards a version of modernity which places primary emphasis upon core values of love and care as foundational. He warns us that while the possibility of impending catastrophes could make changes possible that seem impossible today, as they seemed when humanity was inspired to construct democratic forms of government, a positive outcome for humanity is by no means a certainty. He warns us that we must fundamentally reimagine the defining human priorities that we set for ourselves. He is telling us that the present moment in human history is pivotal and fraught with profound existential risks.

James Merikangas introduces us to the terrifying world of nuclear blackmail in his brief but certainly poignant chapter. Unlike policies of mutually assured destruction, nuclear blackmail can be relied upon to reverse battlefield losses that a nation is enduring by invoking the threat of nuclear escalation. For Wood, Merikangas's conception of nuclear blackmail elicits an image of a room full of armed people with loaded, holstered guns, one of whom pulls his gun out and threatens to shoot one of the others unless he gets his way. Merikangas characterizes the actor in this scenario, Vladimir Putin, as a man who can act as he does – raising the threat of nuclear action – because he is devoid of conscience. He invites us to consider that who Putin has become is likely a confluence of a variety of different forces, including biological ones, that we still don't adequately understand, but he emphasizes, in the very last sentence of his chapter, that the study of destructive figures like Napoleon, Stalin, Hitler, and Putin "remains important if civilization is to survive the nuclear age."

For Wood, pathocracy – government by dangerous, strongmen figures driven by insatiable appetites, deeply compromised empathy, and a very destructive form of narcissistic pathology – represents a clear and present danger the world must soon find a way to contend with if human survival is to be protected. He would maintain that it is a danger that is growing, as witness the rise in autocracies around the world, and a danger that history tells us has resulted in unimaginable human suffering and ecological damage. He also, simultaneously, recognizes that a variety of cultural and sociopolitical forces both create receptivity to strongman leadership and perpetuation of strongmen regimes and the destructiveness that they create. His view of the world is not divided into two pieces defined by idealization of democratic forms of government and denigration of dictatorships; rather, it embraces the harm and the darkness that we all carry within us that have seemingly greater opportunity to express themselves in the context of pathological leadership. Democracies, of course, can produce their own pathological leaders, as witness, for instance, Donald Trump. They can also enact great harm against the human community consonant with what they believe to be their own best interests, as history tells us again and again. It is quite clear that democracies' deficiencies can be glaring and alarmingly inhumane. Wood would argue that it behooves us to be constantly vigilant of our own human frailties in all the forms that they express themselves. This concern reminds us that we must make ever better efforts to educate ourselves about the human condition so that we can improve our capacity for critical thought and for self-appraisal with the intent we can be more caring towards one another. Part of this vigilance, however, must be directed towards the ease with which we can be seduced by an authoritative other who tells us that he can save us.

Wood also believes that distance assessment can be a viable means of understanding people – perhaps particularly national leaders – who otherwise cannot be assessed and/or who would be deeply resistant to psychological or psychiatric evaluation. That would seem to be true of Vladimir Putin. Any attempts to undertake such an evaluation on an in-person basis could be quite dangerous for the mental health professional who tried to do so, as witness Putin's murderous treatment of the press. Wood agrees with the position that Robert Gordon has taken in his unpublished study: that in person assessment and psychological testing of someone who is psychopathic is immensely problematic, likely to yield distorted findings that would obfuscate efforts to understand the underlying personality one is attempting to make sense of. Wood also agrees with Gordon that it is essential for us to weigh the adequacy of mental functioning of national leaders to ensure that particularly destructive personalities do not cause great harm. Like Gordon, Wood feels that behavioural and interpersonal records provide the means to carry out such assessment.

There is, in fact, a great deal of information available about Putin – thousands of pages of documentation, facts, informed speculation, and supposition – that form the public record biographers, investigative reporters, and historians have compiled – so much, indeed, that one could not read it all. This resource material focuses on the actions Putin has taken in undermining democracy in Russia, the electoral process, the Free Press, the Russian Constitution, and the Duma as well as assassinations he has seemingly been involved with (one of Steven Myers's chapters is entitled "Poison"), his military record, his kleptocracy, his interpersonal relationships, and largely latency age childhood experiences. While someone may be inclined to discredit aspects of this information or others' interpretations of it, there are a lot of hard facts and there is a substantial amount of evidence side-by-side the informed speculation and supposition that these documents provide. And while it may be difficult to identify whether Putin has been responsible in a particular instance for an action that has been taken, there is considerable consensus among the five authors Wood read about much of the information they report, and much of the information (even if you disagree about a particular instance), Wood would maintain, comes together to form a reasonably coherent picture, which is what he has argued in his chapters in this book. As previously noted, he also read Putin's own semi-autobiographical work, *First Person*.

Most psychoanalytic work is propositional, reliant on inferential process and our understanding of relevant concepts. Many people are not able to tell us about their childhood. Wood frequently sees people who are unable to remember much about their early experience before age 10 or even 12. That doesn't mean that one can't work with them. It also doesn't mean that when someone provides a rich record of their early experience, one necessarily trusts or accepts it. Working backwards from defences and observable behaviours through elucidation of anxiety and, finally, identification of core conflicts often helps open doors. In this way, one can begin to discern what the core conflicts or themes are in a given personality, even though one doesn't have direct, credible information about somebody's background.

Wood believes it is immensely important to emphasize that, from his perspective, we must pursue our understanding of very destructive personalities from a position of respect and compassion for the varied forms which the human character can assume. The work being undertaken is not about separating bad people from the rest of humanity, but, rather, about more deeply appreciating the vulnerabilities all of us potentially carry within us that allow us to harm both ourselves and others in terrible ways.

Finally, because of its importance to the discussion of distance assessment, I will now spend a little more time reviewing the work of Robert Gordon and his colleagues than I did in the prologue. The Psychodiagnostic Chart (PDC) was developed in 2012 by Robert M. Gordon and Robert F. Borstein to codify the highly complex Psychodynamic Diagnostic Manual (PDM). They later updated the PDC (Gordon and Bornstein, 2018) for the PDM-2 (Lingiardi and McWilliams, 2017). The PDC-2 is a quick practitioner rating form that may be used for diagnoses, treatment formulations, progress reports, and outcome assessment, as well as for empirical research on personality. It can be used when the person is not available, and assessment is instead based on documents, records, collateral interviews, or other sources of information. The PDC-2 represents an effective means to carry out meaningful, valid distance assessment of people who, by virtue of the position of power they occupy, may profoundly affect the lives of millions of people.

Research by Gordon and Stoffey (2014) and Gordon and Bornstein (2018) show excellent validity of the original PDC and the updated PDC-2.

The Mental Functions Scales used in Gordon's unpublished study are part of the overall PDC-2. They have high test–retest reliability (0.77 to 0.89, all p values are less than 0.001). Interrater reliability correlations range from 0.82 to 0.92 (Gordon and Bornstein, 2018). Additionally, to date there are 32 studies that support the clinical utility and validity of the PDCs. (https://sites.google.com/site/psychodiagnosticchart/)

Gordon argues that the 12 mental functions could be readily understood by experienced psychoanalytic practitioners and could be applied to the assessment of three state leaders: Volodymyr Zelenskyy, Vladimir Putin, and Donald Trump. Moreover, he felt that the Mental Functions Scale provided meaningful assessment of an array of essential mental functions that would be critical for anyone to possess who was in a position of leadership of a large national body. Using 50 experienced psychodynamic practitioners, he demonstrated that the Mental Functions Scale appeared to be capable of producing distinctive portraits of each of the three men that set each of them apart from the others. Asserting that "the Mental Functions Scale gives us a measure of a continuum of strengths and weaknesses on a full array of all the main psychological functions" (quote taken from his unpublished study), he reported that Trump scored significantly lower than Putin on all of the 12 mental functions and that both men scored significantly lower than Zelenskyy had. He typified Putin and Trump as the scoring in the "dangerous" range on all 12 mental functions while Zelenskyy's high score was thought to be indicative of a "healthy leader" (p. 12). Scores were expressed as percentages of an idealized level of functioning (100%), which Gordon felt rendered public appreciation of score meaning much more transparent. He estimated that scores of less than 70% ought to disqualify a given candidate for consideration for public office.

In the context of Gordon's unpublished study, it would appear that the PDC-2 shows promise for future distance assessment of people who occupy critical leadership positions. As such, his work and the work of his colleagues may offer us the means to assess level of functioning in leaders with a standardized instrument possessed of reliability, validity, and utility without entailing the necessity of face-to-face examination, which may, for a variety of reasons, not be possible to undertake. Wood believes that possessing such means in a world where violent, autocratic leadership has accounted for unimaginable human calamities is potentially essential for our survival as a species.

Taken together, the distance methodologies that Wood and Willock used and the distance assessment instrument that Gordon and others have developed – particularly if further study confirms their viability – may offer us the means to establish the convergent validity of these two forms of distance assessment. That is, should we be able to demonstrate that the two distance assessment methodologies being referenced here produce a high level of agreement in their appraisal of leadership personalities, we may feel we can invest greater confidence in the portraits they provide us than the results of either assessment methodology considered on its own. Much like the approach that Gordon and his group developed, the methodology which Willock and Wood used, although very familiar to most depth clinicians, will require considerable further study, however, before its applicability can be confirmed in the assessment of dangerous leaders. It is my hope that works like this volume will inspire vigorous discussion within the psychological professions that further extends our understanding of distance assessment investigation.

References

Beck, U. (2016). *The metamorphosis of the world: How climate change is transforming our concept of the world.* New York, John Wiley & Sons.

Byrne, E. (2021). *Why the metaphor of complementary dualism, and metaphor itself, are foundational to achieving sustainability.* In Metaphor, Sustainability, Transformation (pp. 119–136). Routledge.

Gordon, R.M., & Bornstein, R.F. (2018). Construct validity of the Psychodiagnostic Chart: A transdiagnostic measure of personality organization, personality syndromes, mental functioning, and symptomatology. *Psychoanalytic Psychology*, 35(2), 280–288. https://doi.org/10.1037/pap0000142

Gordon, R.M., & Stoffey, R.W. (2014) Operationalizing the psychodynamic diagnostic manual: A preliminary study of the psychodiagnostics chart. *Bulletin of the Menninger Clinic, 78*, 1–15.

Lingiardi, V., & McWilliams, N. (Eds.). (2017). Psychodynamic diagnostic manual: PDM- 2 (2nd ed.). Hoboken, New Jersey, The Guilford Press.

Epilogue

Richard Wood

I deliberated about writing the epilogue the reader is about to encounter, deciding, in the end, that it was appropriate to share my concerns. It is important to emphasize that the views which the epilogue espouses are my own and do not represent a consensus opinion of the five authors who contributed to this book.

I do not see a peace treaty in Ukraine as either the answer or as even possible unless it served some transactional end for Putin. I do not think Putin is invested in ending the war with Ukraine, believing, as I do, that a long war will allow Putin to weaponize refugees, economies, energy, and food so that he can destabilize democracies. That, I foresee, is the real strategic aim of Putin's war: deconstructing democracy.

This is essentially the position that the four of the major biographers I reviewed seemed to take as well. Framed within a popular, contemporary literary metaphor, Putin can be seen to experience his struggle with democracy as an existential crisis and, kind of like Harry Potter and Voldemort, feels that neither can live while the other survives. Put differently, this is a zero-sum game for Putin: either he endures, or the other guy does. The bullying will only stop if he feels that it is to his advantage to do so. I believe that is and must be the nature of the relationship between ambitious autocracies and ambitious democracies. Decency and cooperation are not desirable answers in and of themselves for Putin unless they serve his perceived self-interest. He would, however, make a considerable effort to simulate these qualities if he thought it would work well for him to do so. Any peace treaty would always be subject to compromise as soon as Putin's feral intelligence identifies opportunities to exploit the other.

These beliefs are very strongly held. I would love to believe in diplomatic solutions but I don't think they're possible any more than they were possible when dealing with a personality like Hitler's or Stalin's. Alexander J. Motyl, writing in *Politico* on March 14 of last year, makes a similar point, arguing that both Hitler and Putin are fascists and that

> in this scheme of things, Putin's invasion of Ukraine is equivalent to Hitler's attack on Austria, Czechoslovakia, or Poland … Russia will be either aggressive and victorious or aggressive and humiliated. Either way, the war in Ukraine is not the end of the West's troubles with Putin.

Motyl is a professor in political science at Rutgers specializing in Soviet and post-Soviet era politics.

The implications of this understanding of Putin suggests that the only effective way to stop him and bring peace to the region is through a resolute demonstration of force on the part of the West. Tragically, more war and more horror and more brinksmanship and threat from Putin. In opposing Putin, the West, however, must be willing to counteract Putin's ultimate strategic aim: destabilizing democracy and replacing it with populist movements that he nurtures. In order to protect democracy, the West will have to address its fundamental weaknesses: wealth inequality, its handling of immigration (taking steps to ensure that new immigrants are given the best chance to successfully integrate themselves into their new societies), and its energy dependence on Russia. If Russia does indeed intend to create widespread starvation in Africa as a means of generating more immigrants for the West to deal with, it will be essential for the West to address African food insufficiency with more determination than it has in the past, not only in response to pressing humanitarian need (which one hopes would be irresistibly compelling in and of itself), but also out of self-interest.

The downside of opposing Russia and undercutting Europe's energy dependence on it is that one is effectively pushing Russia towards greater interdependence on other autocratic nations, but I would argue that such a shift is an inevitable consequence of the differing aims and intentionalities of democracies versus autocracies. The greatest danger is a nuclear one: as Putin finds himself contained and/or defeated by a Ukraine supported by Western weaponry, particularly if his sense of authority and grandiosity is successfully compromised, it is conceivable that he may respond to the immense measure of subjective threat that he experiences as an unbearable catastrophic event, unleashing weapons of mass destruction in response – much as Hitler did in reaction to Germany's impending defeat when he ordered Germany's essential industrial infrastructure to be destroyed at the end of World War II. The argument that Hitler used was a Darwinian one: if Germany was not strong enough to dominate other nations, it didn't deserve to survive – which is to say that if Hitler's own survival was compromised, so must Germany's. As Motyl points out, Hitler conflated his own sense of identity with Germany's, just as Putin does with Russia. In this fashion, a powerful personal sense of disintegration impels an autocratic leader to extend his own personal devastation into the lives of all the people he can touch with his actions.

While I anticipate that negotiating a way towards a meaningful and lasting peace through the bargaining table is very unlikely, I feel it is essential that both sides continue to talk to each other. For the West, that means negotiating from an "eyes wide open" position – one that holds the realities and improbabilities of negotiation with Putin in the very forefront of one's mind.

Like Motyl, I do not see NATO expansion as a primary cause for the war in Ukraine, though I would acknowledge that the US has clearly broken some of its promises to Putin in this regard. It is also true, simultaneously, that Putin has consistently broken his implied promises to the West to democratize Russia. I think that it can be argued that once the West finally recognized Putin's autocratic nature shortly before the end of his first ten years of rule, it had good cause to be concerned about the threat which Putin presented, if not well before that time. Ironically, of course, Putin's aggressive actions in Chechnya, Georgia, Syria, and in Crimea could only be expected to further consolidate NATO's appreciation that Putin represented potential jeopardy for NATO nations. As stated earlier, I do not consider that the real aim of the invasion of Ukraine in February 2022 was the conquest of Ukraine; rather, it was a means through which Putin could disrupt and destabilize Western democracies.

Reference

Motyl, Alexander J. (2022). *Opinion|Putin Isn't Just an Autocrat. He's Something Worse*. https://www.politico.com/news/magazine/2022/03/14/lets-call-putin-fascist-autocrat-00016982

Index

Note: Page numbers followed by "n" denote endnotes.

Abrahamic religions 103–104
accountability 47, 51
accountable democratic government 96
Adorno, Theodor: *The Authoritarian Personality* 83
Adverse Childhood Event 59
adverse childhood experiences (ACEs) 54
Alexievich, Svetlana 75; *Second-Hand Time* 73
Alyukov, Maxim 72, 77n3
anxiety 61, 105, 112
Arendt, Hannah 72, 76, 83, 108
atomic bombs 101
The Authoritarian Personality (Adorno) 83
autocracy 84, 90
autocratic leadership 108, 109, 113

"bad" war 89
Balint, Michael 67
Beck, U. 98, 99, 110
Beyond the Pleasure Principle (Freud) 55
Biden, Joe 94
blame: and collective guilt 69; conscious misattribution of 9; and truth 71–73
blame shifting 9, 45–49, 107; projective identification and 10
Blueberry Hill 53, 54, 67
Blue Stream 58
Bolsonaro, Jair 94, 109
Borderline Personality Organization 3
Borisenko, V. 19, 20, 38
Borovik, Artyom 56
Borstein, Robert F. 112
British Object Relations group 60
brutality: and power 33; and ruthlessness 28

Burkle, F.M. 1
Bush, George W. 53–54
Byrne, E. 109

capitalism 93, 94, 109
character structure 16
Chechen war 22
Chechnya 69; destructive behavior in 63; physical war 89
childhood adversity 54–55
chosen myth 73–76
chosen traumas 71, 107
Cold War 101, 102
collective guilt 76–77; blame and 69
Columbus, Christopher 93
communism 95, 102
compassion 88, 89
complex posttraumatic stress disorder (CPTSD) 5
compulsive greed 97
constitutional autocracy 75
Contemporary Relational Psychoanalysis 53
contrivance: and impulsivity 45; and intimacy 36–44
Covington, Coline 107, 108, 110
Crimea: invasion of 74–75; Russian acts of aggression 76
cruelty: compromised empathy and 28–33; and rapacity 109; and risk-taking 8
cynicism 9, 89

Dabrowski, K. 83
"The Dangerous Case of Donald Trump" (Post) 82
Daudov, Rustam 57–59

120 Index

Deaton, Angus 92
decency 87, 88
delusions 64; functions of 63–64
democracy 48, 93, 94, 96, 111, 116;
    development of 98; and equality 92
Depressive Position 60, 66
Die Zeit 59
dissent, tolerance of 95
dissociated self-states 59, 61
distrust of information 72
distrust of propaganda 72
diverse identities 53
Dobbert, S. 57, 59
Dodes, L. 2, 3, 9
Dzihic (Serbian scholar) 72, 108

economic development, benefits of 92–93
economic hardship 54
Eichmann, Adolf 83
elevated risk tolerance 27
Eltchaninoff, Michael 32, 39
emancipatory catastrophism 98, 110
empathy 89; and cruelty 28–33
equality: and human rights 96; between
    men and women 97; principle of 96
Europe: energy dependence 116; plan for
    32; war in 31, 102

Fairbairn, W.R.D. 61, 62
false flags 70, 76
Faustian bargain 86, 90, 109
fear 84, 85, 87–90
fear-drenched environment 27, 88, 109
First Person: An Astonishingly Frank Self?
    Portrait by Russia's President (Putin)
    17, 20–23, 30, 42, 48, 56, 112
food, shortages of 28–31
Freud, S. 63, 64; *Beyond the Pleasure*
    Principle 55
Friedman, H.J. 2
Fromm, E. 13, 79–83
fundraising event 53

Gartner, J.D. 2
genocide 55, 64, 70, 93, 98
Gessen, Masha 18, 24, 28, 29, 33–35, 38,
    40, 41, 44, 49, 90
Ghosh, Amitav 94
Gogol, N.: *The Government Inspector* 77n2
Goldfarb, Alex 34
Gordon, R.M. 5, 50–51, 111–113
Gosnell, Jack 37

The Government Inspector (Gogol) 77n2
grandiosity 84, 86
Great Patriotic War 70
Greenacre, Phyllis 83
Greene, G. 77; *The Quiet American* 76
group narcissism 79
"group self" concept 81
Gumilev, Lev 74, 75
Guntrip, H. 59, 61, 62, 64–66, 105, 107
Gusinski, Vladimir 33–34

hallucination 64
Hay, Barbara 36
The Heart of Man 1
Herzen, Alexander: *Who's to Blame* 71
hierarchical structures 28
Hiroshima 101, 102
Hitler, A. 13, 55, 60–61, 70, 71, 77n1,
    101–104, 110, 115, 116
homosexuality 46–47
Hughes, I. 3, 8, 82, 109
humanity 83, 84, 88, 109; in form of
    dissociation 88; history of 96; modernity
    as 92; recovery of 89
human rights: equality and 96; legal
    protection for 99
hyper-masculine posture 28
hypermasculinity 97–98

"ideal hungry personality" 83
identity: malignant narcissistic 13; national
    48, 107, 108; personal 23, 43, 48; state
    23, 43
The Ignorance or How We Produce the Evil
    (Miller) 55
Illarionov, Andrei 35
Ilyin, Ivan 35, 74, 75, 78n9
impulsivity 44–45; contrivance and 45; and
    recklessness 51
"incestuous symbiosis" 79
Industrial Revolution 92
injury/grievance 43; narcissistic 3, 90, 108;
    scope of 33
inner life 49–52
insight-oriented therapy 66
interpersonal relationships 8, 14, 59, 111
intimacy 5, 7, 40; contrivance and 36–44

Judo culture 21

Kernberg, O. 1–3, 13, 51, 62, 80–82
Khordorkovsky, Mikhail 35

Index 121

Kiselyov, Dmitry 77
Klein, Melanie 59, 60
kleptocracy 33, 89, 97, 111
Kohut, H. 3, 66, 81

Langer, Walter 103
leader-follower relationship 79–90, 108
Lenin, V. 74
liberal representative democracy 98, 99
London, bombings of 101

Macron, Emmanuel 63
malignant narcissism 1, 2, 79; brutality
    and power 33; characteristics of
    13–14, 19; contrivance and intimacy
    36–44; as defence against borderline
    fragmentation 3; features of 13, 17–18;
    formulation of 4; inner life 49–52;
    working model of 105
malignant narcissist 11, 12; devastated
    internal life 10; life posture 6
malignant narcissistic leadership 80–82, 84
Malkin, C. 2
Mao 55
Marshall Plan 102
masculine domination 97
materialism 97, 98, 110
McWilliams, N. 61
meat contract 29
media distrust, in silencing civil dissent
    77n4
Media-Most 33
media trust 72
Mental Functions Scales 112, 113
Merikangas, James 110
Mika, E. 2, 3, 11, 82
Milevsky, Avidan 61
Milgram, Stanley 83
militarism, dynamic of 97
Miller, Alice: *The Ignorance or How We
    Produce the Evil* 55
Millon, Theodore 61
"mirror hungry personality" 83
mistrust 6–8, 10, 12; personal threat
    and 81; and profound suspicion 50;
    solipsism and 43
modernity 109; accountable democratic
    government 96; destructive forces of
    109; equality and human rights 96; as
    humanity 92; metamorphosis of 98–100;
    narrative of 99; pathologies of 96–98;
    science and reason 95; strengths and

pathologies of 94–95; tales of 92–94;
    tolerance of dissent 95
Modi, N. 94, 109
Motyl, Alexander J. 116; *Politico* 115
mutually assured destruction 101, 102
Myers, S.L. 19–22, 25, 38, 39, 42, 43,
    45–46

Nagasaki 101, 102
Napoleon 71, 102, 104, 110
narcissism 75; malignant (*see* malignant
    narcissism); pathological 1, 79
narcissistic defences 3
narcissistic leadership, pathological forms
    of 82
National Health Service (NHS) 5
national identity 48, 107, 108
National Socialism 95
NATO countries 69, 70, 77, 117
Navalny, Alexei 97
Nazis 46, 54, 55, 64, 65
Newton, I. 94
nuclear blackmail 101–104
nurturance 8

Object Relations Theory 59
omnipotence 84, 86, 88
"On Leadership" 82
openness 85, 87
Operation Starfish Prime 102

"Paranoia and Charisma" (Robbins) 83
paranoid delusions 63
paranoid leader 80, 81
Paranoid-Schizoid Position 59, 60
parent-child relationship 41
passionarnost 75, 76, 107
pathocracy 110
pathological leadership 98–100, 111;
    receptivity to 86
pathological narcissism 1, 79
Pavlovsky, Gleb 22
PDC-2 112, 113
perpetual combat 11, 12
perpetual war footing 12
personal identity 23, 43, 48
personality disorders 98–99
Peter the Great 75
Pickering, Tom 37
pleonexia 33
Politico (Motyl) 115
"politics of eternity" 74

122 Index

"politics of inevitability" 74
Post, Jerrold: "The Dangerous Case of Donald Trump" 82
posttraumatic stress disorder (PTSD) 5
power: brutality and 33; and domination 7; of economic growth 92; hierarchy of 97; prerogatives of 31
projective identification 10, 45–49, 107
psychoanalytic theory 16
psychoanalytic therapy 66
Psychodiagnostic Chart (PDC) 112
Psychodynamic Diagnostic Manual (PDM) 112
psychodynamics 2, 17, 27
psychological dynamics 13
psychological literature 12
psychopathy: literature on 27; narcissistic 2; subclass of 4
psychotherapeutic assessment 50–51
psychotherapy, public acceptance and destigmatization of 66
"a psychotic spiral" 2
Putina, Maria Ivanovna 56, 57
Putin, V. 1, 16, 17, 25, 53, 69, 85, 94, 98, 102–105, 109–111, 113, 115–117; attitude towards remorse 31; behaviour as fund of information 17; Borisenko's appraisal of 20; callous killer 59–61; childhood 105; coda 67; commitment to combative life stance 19; compromised empathy and cruelty 28–33; contrivance and intimacy 36–44; destruction of voice 33–36; elevated risk tolerance 27; experiences of childhood adversity 54–55; *First Person: An Astonishingly Frank Self? Portrait by Russia's President* 17, 20–23, 30, 42, 48, 112; hope for likes of 65–67; impulsivity and recklessness 44–45; inner life 49–52; investment in brutality and ruthlessness 28; message in speech 70; mother 56–59; obsession with material wealth 97; parentage 106; projective identification, splitting, and blame shifting 45–49; strength of character 21; televised appraisal of war 24; vision and threats 77; war of aggression in Ukraine 73; weighting and appraisal of historical events 18
Putin, Vladimir Spiridonovich 56, 57
Puttkamer, Eberhardt von 37–38

The Quiet American (Greene) 76

racism 76, 93, 99
Ratner, Austin 86
reason 12; science and 12, 95
recklessness 44–45; impulsivity and 51
Redlich, Fritz 103
repetition compulsion 55
risk-taking: combat and 11; cruelty and 8
Robbins, Robert: "Paranoia and Charisma" 83
Roldugin, Sergei 21
rule-based international order 96–97
Russia: energy dependence on 116; homosexuals in 46; invasions of 71; political dynamics and rationale of 69
Russian Constitution 105, 111
Russian Federation 90
Russo, Antonio 57, 58

sadism 7, 9
safety 6, 86, 88; in fear-drenched environment 109
Salye, Marina 28–29
Sarkozy, Nicolas 25
schizoid, defined as 61
schizoid egos 65
schizoid personalities 61–65, 105
schizoid suicide 62
Schreber, Daniel Paul 63, 64
science and reason 12, 95
Scientific Revolution 92
Second-Hand Time (Alexievich) 73
Sedelmayer, France 37
separation/divorce 54
Shaw, D. 2, 3
Short, Philip 19–25, 30, 36–39, 41
Smith, Adam 94
Snyder, T. 31, 35, 74, 76, 107
Sobchak (Mayor) 29, 36, 43
social narcissism 79
social violence 80
solipsism 12; and mistrust 43
Soviet Union 69, 74, 99; dissolution of 73
'special military operation' 55
splitting 10, 45–49
Stalin, J. 55, 74, 102, 104, 110, 115
starvation 8
state identity 23, 43
Stevens, J.E. 54, 55
Stiernlof, Sture 36–37
Stoffey, R.W. 112

stoicism 27
strongmen leaders 94–95
A Study of Malignant Narcissism: Personal and Professional Insights 1

Tansey, M.J. 2
tolerance, of dissent 95
transactional motivation 10
trauma 106; balance between congenital and 27; repetitive nature of 55; in repetitive patterns 16
trauma-driven behaviour 16
trauma-informed character structure 16
traumatizing narcissism 2
Treaty of Versailles 101
Trump, D. 94, 109, 111, 113
truth 56, 57; blame and 71–73

Ukraine: conflict in 31–32; invasion of 69, 70, 74–75, 77, 77n5, 94, 117; management of war in 45; Nazis in 46; neo-Nazis in 70; peace treaty in 115; physical war 89; Putin's narrative of aggression 77n1; Putin's war of aggression in 73; Russian acts of aggression 76; sovereignty of 74; 'special military operation' 55; war in 51, 76, 77
United States 94, 101; war in Europe 102

United States Department of Veterans Affairs (VA) 5
Universal Declaration of Human Rights 99
U.S. Center for Disease Control and Prevention 54

violence 96–97
voice, destruction of 33–36
vulgarisms 44
vulnerability 55; and depreciation 84; and fear 71; sense of 84; strength and intolerance of 19–28

Who's to Blame (Herzen) 71
Willock, B. 105–107, 113
Wink, Walter 96
Winnicott, D.W. 60, 65
Wood, R. 105–113
World War I 101
World War II 18, 26, 30, 54, 55, 101, 102, 116

Xi Jinping 94

Yavlinsky, Grigory 46
Yeltsin, B. 22, 24

Zelenskyy, Volodymyr Oleksandrovych 61, 113

Printed in the United States
by Baker & Taylor Publisher Services